INDUCEMENT CYCLES

Ebook 2.00

INDUCEMENT CYCLES

Introduction

Manipulation in prices in the forex market is a violation of the terms of agreement between two or more parties. It is a form of market manipulation that seeks to benefit one party at the expense of another. Manipulation in the forex market can be done in various ways, such as false rumors, false statements, and price manipulation. It can also be done by trading on inside information or by using high-frequency trading algorithms. It is important to be aware of the potential risks of manipulation in the forexmarket, as it can have serious legal and financial consequences.

TRADING in the financial markets can be a profitable endeavor, but it also carries certain risks. One of these risks is the potential for manipulation of prices by banks andother financial institutions. This type of manipulation can have a significant effect on themarkets, as it can cause prices to move in an unnatural direction. In this book, we will explore the different types of manipulation that can occur in the financial markets, and how they can be prevented. We will examine the different techniques used by banks and other financial institutions to manipulate prices, and how TRADERS AND INVESTORS can protect themselves from these practices. By understanding the different types of manipulation, investors AND TRADERS can be better informed andmore aware of potential risks in the financial markets.

MARKET

The basis of the trade to buy cheap and sell expensive is to purchase products or anything at a lower cost than their market value and then resell them at a higher price. This is a common strategy employed by many businesses, as it allows them to make a profit on the difference between the purchase and sale prices. By buying products at a lower cost than they are worth, businesses can maximize their profits. This strategy can be used in any market, including stocks, commodities, real estate, and digital assets.

The trade buy cheap and sell expensive is a fundamental concept in trading, investment, and entrepreneurship. It is based on the idea of buying low and selling high, which is a basic principle of economics. This strategy involves finding undervalued assets and then reselling them at a higher price, thus making a profit. This strategy can be used to both generate income and grow capital. By buying low and selling high, investors can increase their returns and build wealth over time. However, it is important to remember that buying low and selling high is not a guarantee of success. The success of this strategy depends on the Investor's knowledge and ability to identify undervalued assets and then resell them at the right time.

THAT WHY WE NEED STRUCTURE TO KNOW IF THE PRICE CHEAP OR EXPENSIVE

FORGET THE DIRECTION OR U NEED TO KNOW THE DIRECTION TO TRADE THAT DISTRACT YOUR FOCUS

Distracting your focus in trading can lead to making poor decisions and can be detrimental to your success. To minimize distractions, it is important to create a trading plan and stick to it. This plan should include setting specific goals, identifying risk levels, and determining when to enter and exit trades.
Additionally, it is important to limit the amount of time you spend on the markets and avoid making trades when feeling emotional. Additionally, it is important to take regular breaks and step away from the markets when you feel overwhelmed or are not able to focus. Finally, it is important to stay informed on the markets By creating and following a trading plan, you can minimize distractions and increase your chances of success.

It is not necessary to know the direction of the markets in order to be successful in INTRADAY TRADING. While having some knowledge of the markets and their direction can be helpful, it is not essential. Successful INTRADAY trading and

more on understanding the risks and rewards associated with different trades, and having a strategy for managing those risks. Additionally, it is important to have an understanding of TIME and technical aspects of the markets.

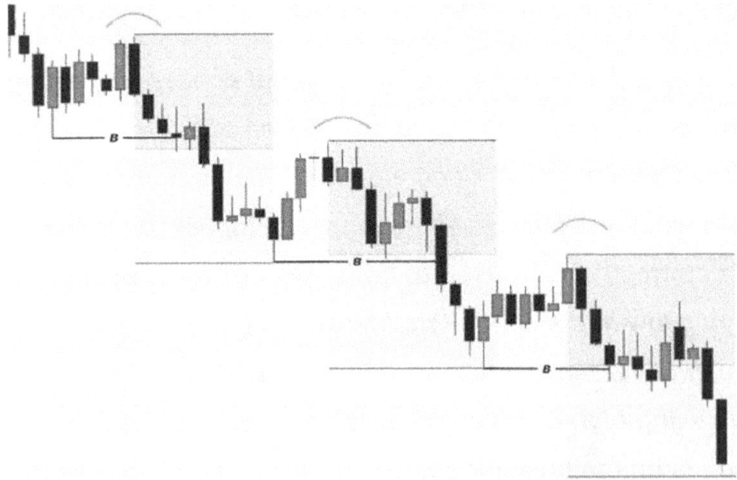

MARKET PHASES

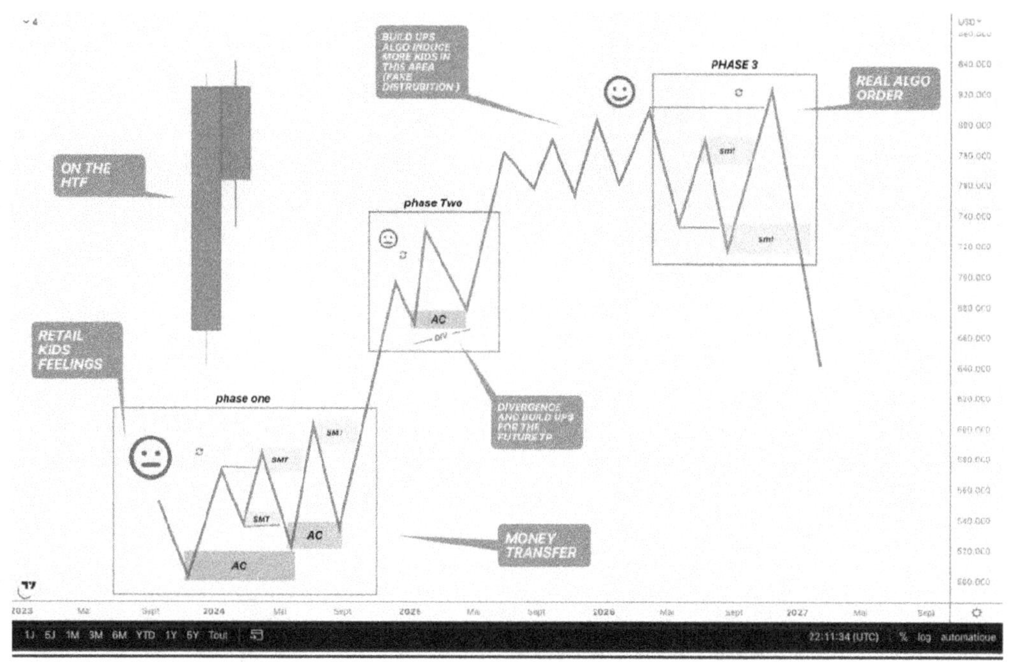

**PHASE ONE OF STRUCTURE MONEY TRANSFER**

**PHASE TWO PROTECTING THE ORDERS**

**FAKE REVERSAL**

PHASE THREE TRAPPING MORE PPL

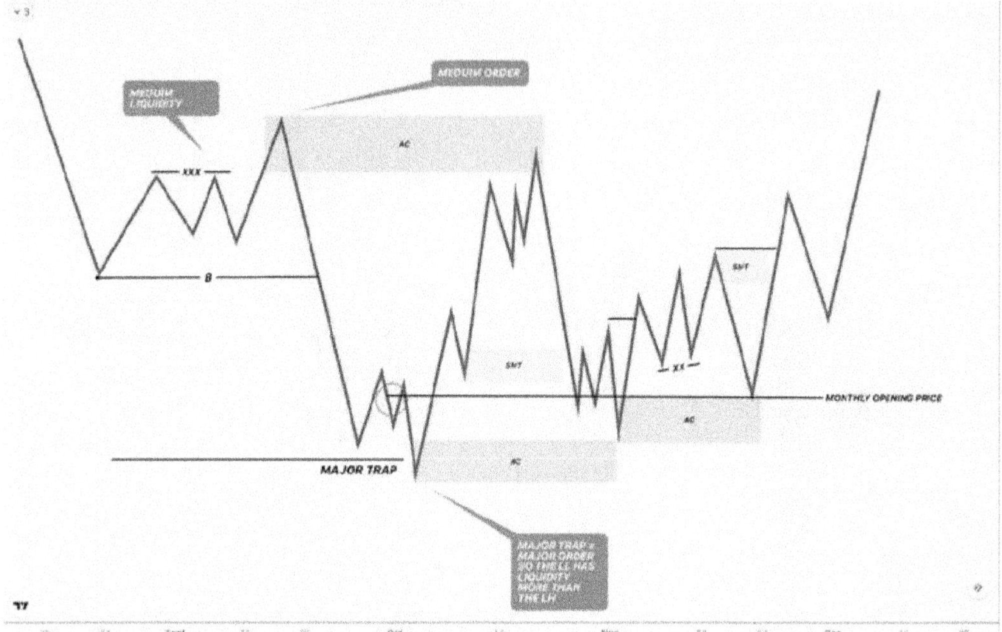

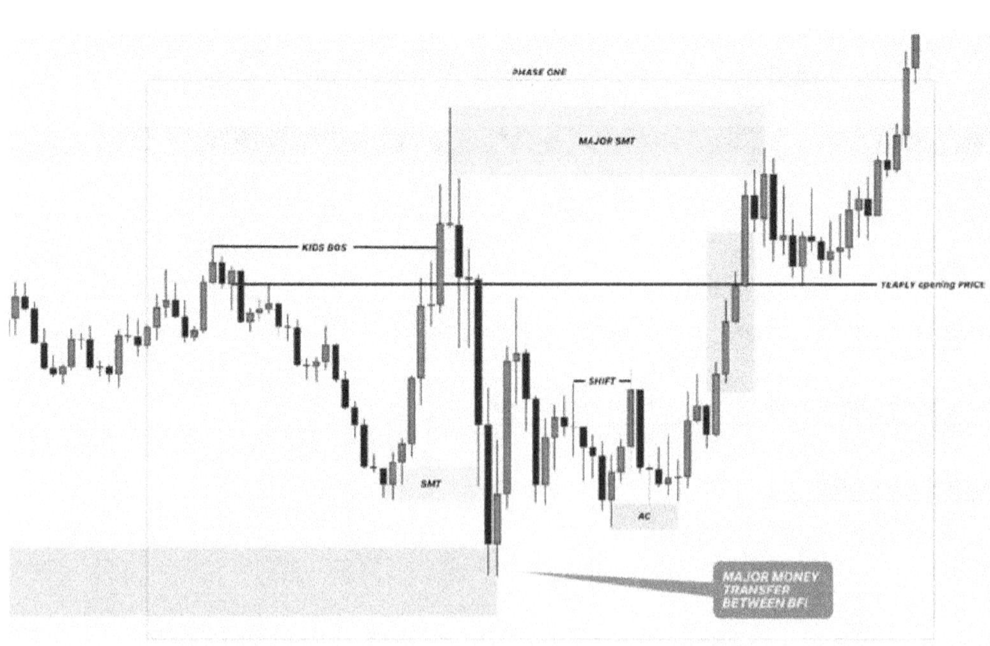

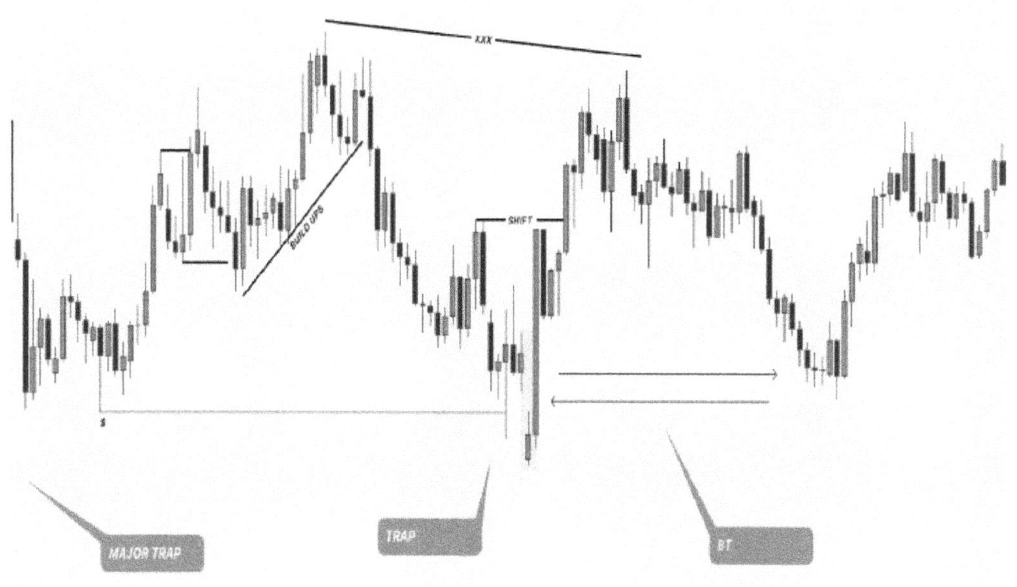

MAJOR TRAP + MEDIUM/MINOR TRAP + CHC WITH IMB = BETWEEN MONEY TRANSFER

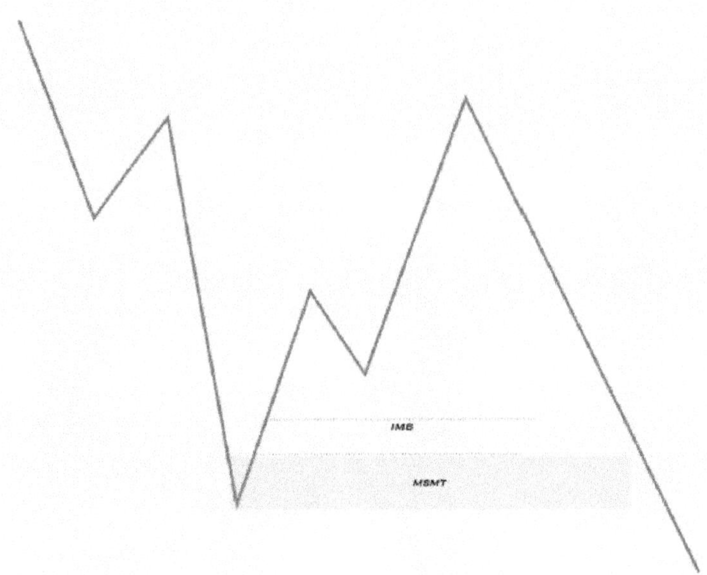

EXTERNAL TRAP

THE FIRST THING WE WILL DO, IS WAIT FOR A MAJOR TRAP IN THE MARKET. THEN WE WILL CHANGE THE TIME FRAME TO LTF DIRECTLY.

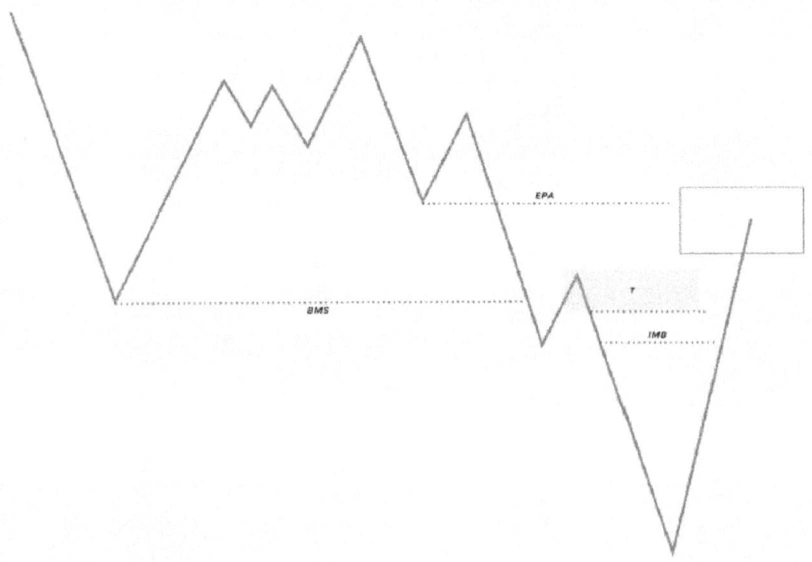

ENTRY MODELS

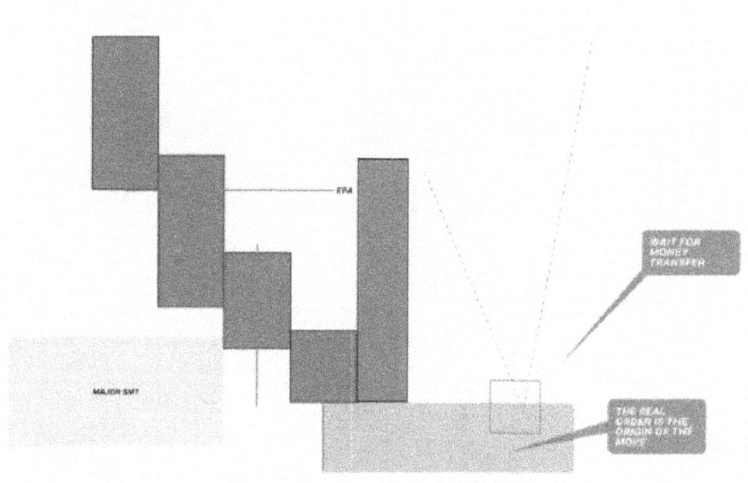

TYPE 1

LTF entry confirmation.

The order that cause the EPA is the real order. This Method is another type of Shift or Change of character.

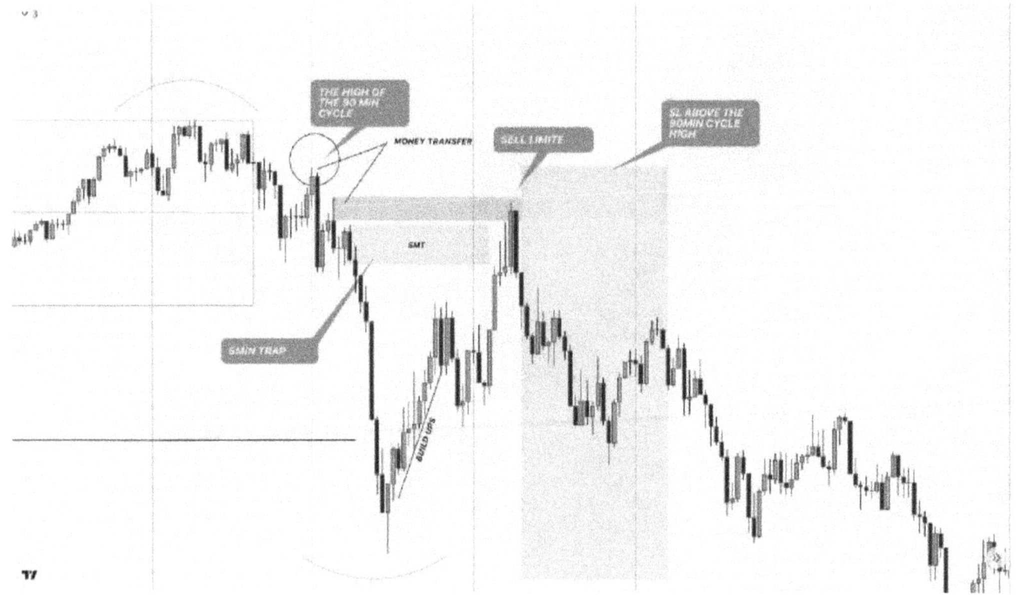

TYPE 2

Entry with Limit Order.

The real order is in the 90m cycle high, fake one is below the 90min cycle opening price.

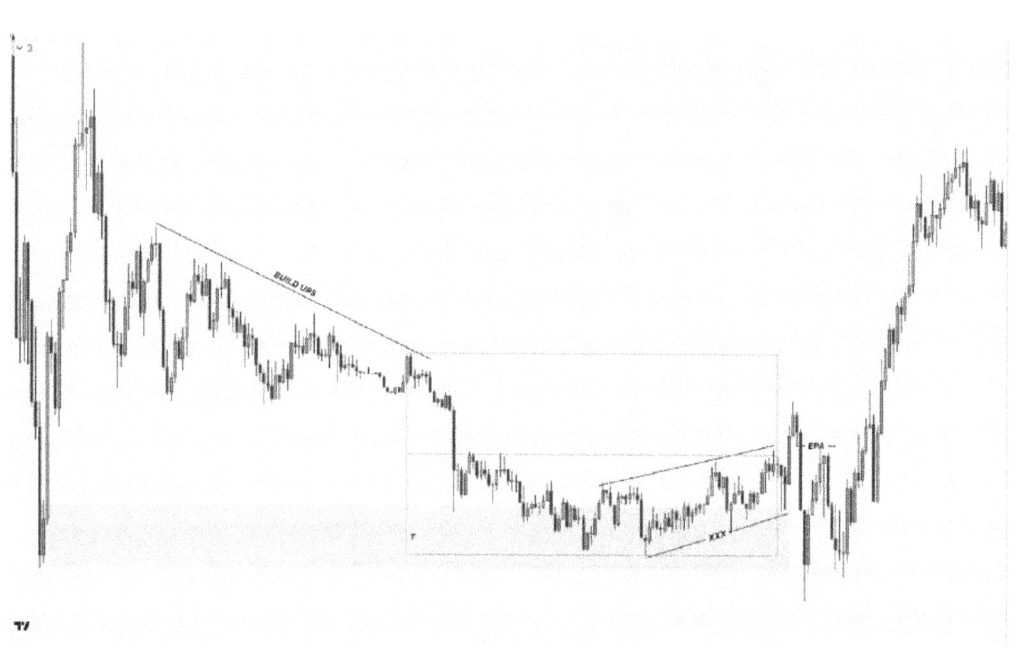

3MIN

NOTE:
When you try to find the order that cause the EPA, start from HTF like 5m,
then 3, 2m, and 1m. Remember that TRAPS are everywhere.

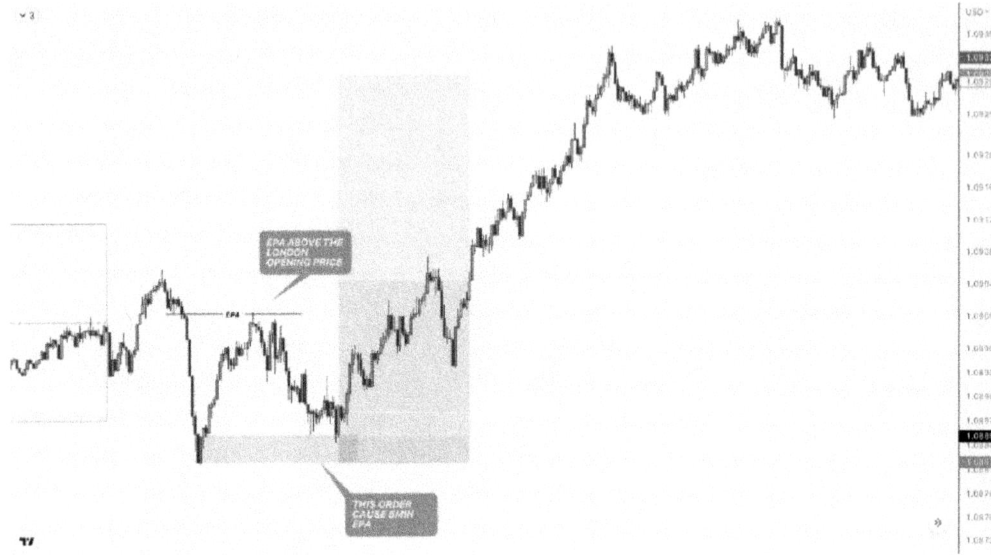
EPA ABOVE THE LONDON OPENING PRICE
EPA
THIS ORDER CAUSE BMH EPA

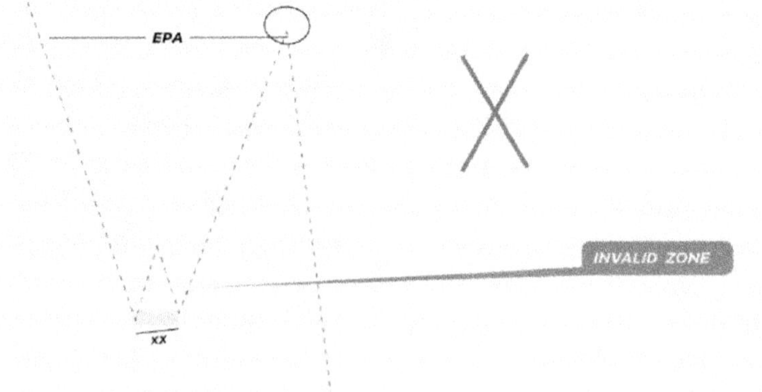
EPA
INVALID ZONE
XX

90MIN CYCLE HIGH
5MIN TRAPN
5MIN EPA
XXX
ASIA MIDLINE
BEAUTIFUL KID TRAP
XXX
90 MIN
TRAP ZONE
5MIN EPA
MT

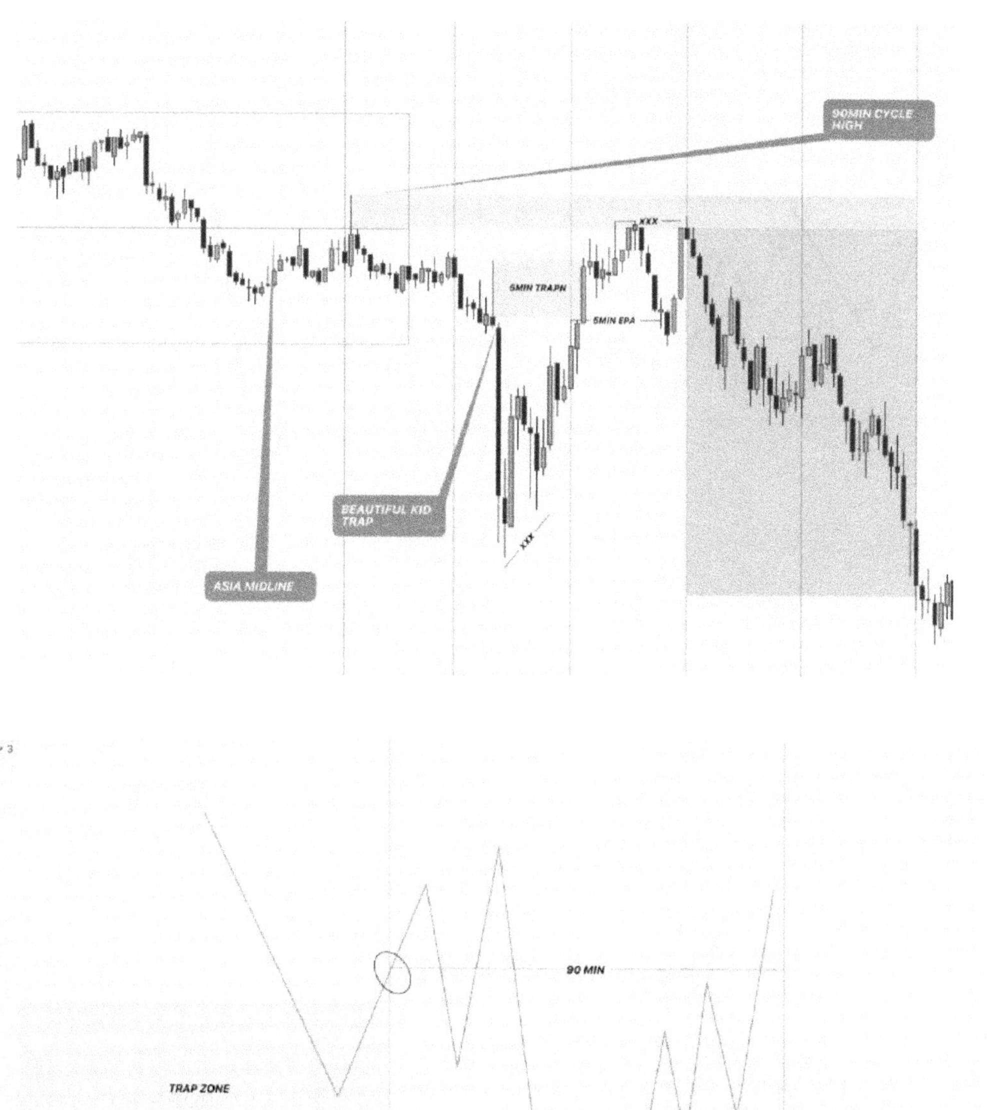

ENTRY MODEL

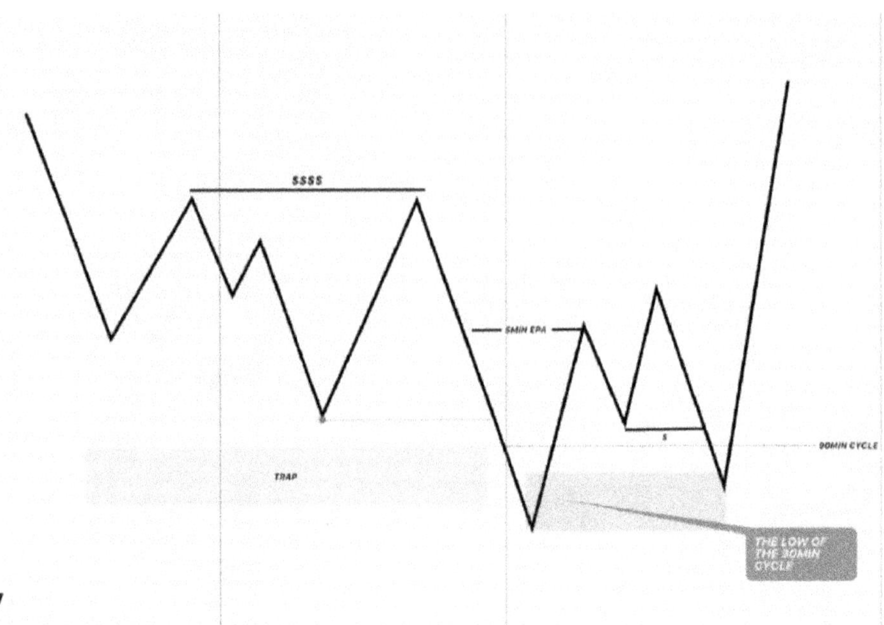
SSSS
5MIN EPA
TRAP
S
30MIN CYCLE
THE LOW OF THE 30MIN CYCLE

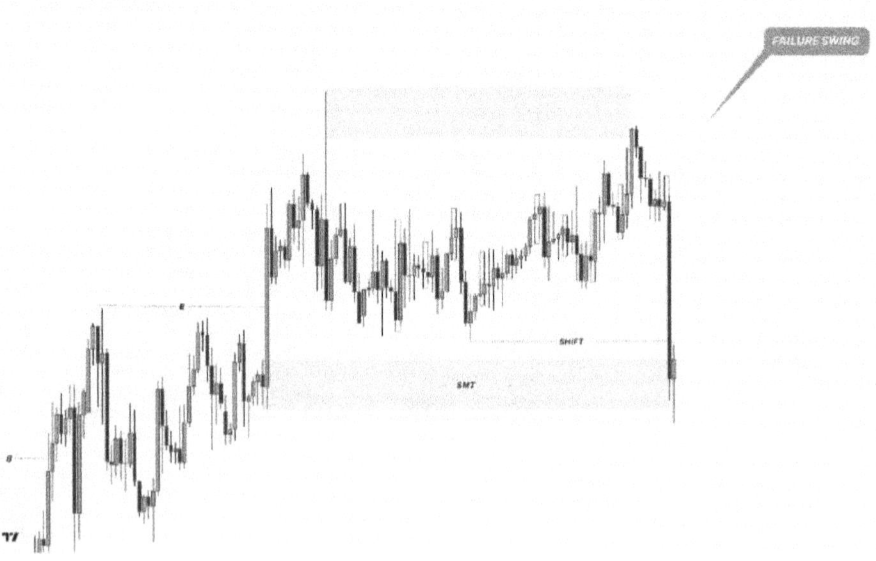
FAILURE SWING
SHIFT
SMT
4H

SECOND
PARTIAL
FIRST PARTIAL
BUILD UP
EPA
THE LOW OF
THE 90 MIN
CYCLE

3M

FAILURE SWING
LOOKING FOR
SELL IN THIS
PREMIUM
AREA.
SHIFT

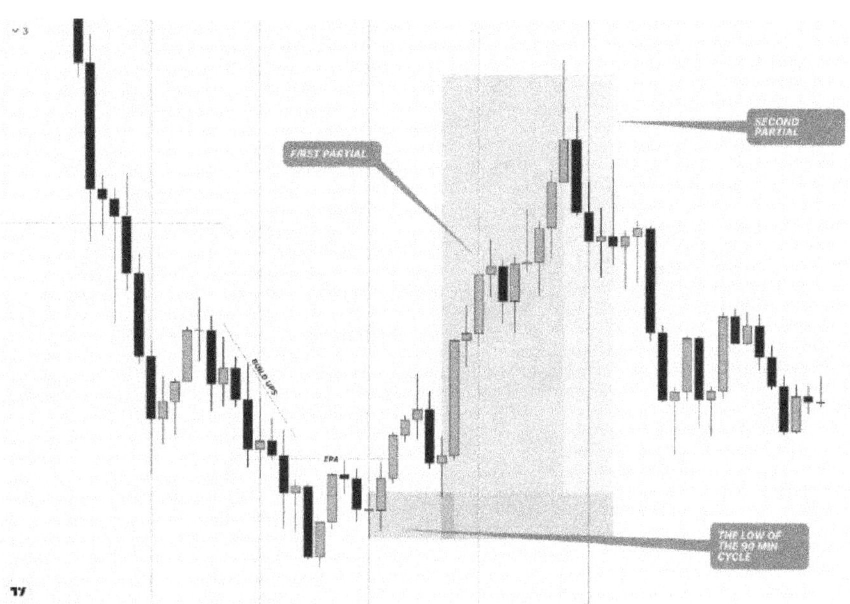

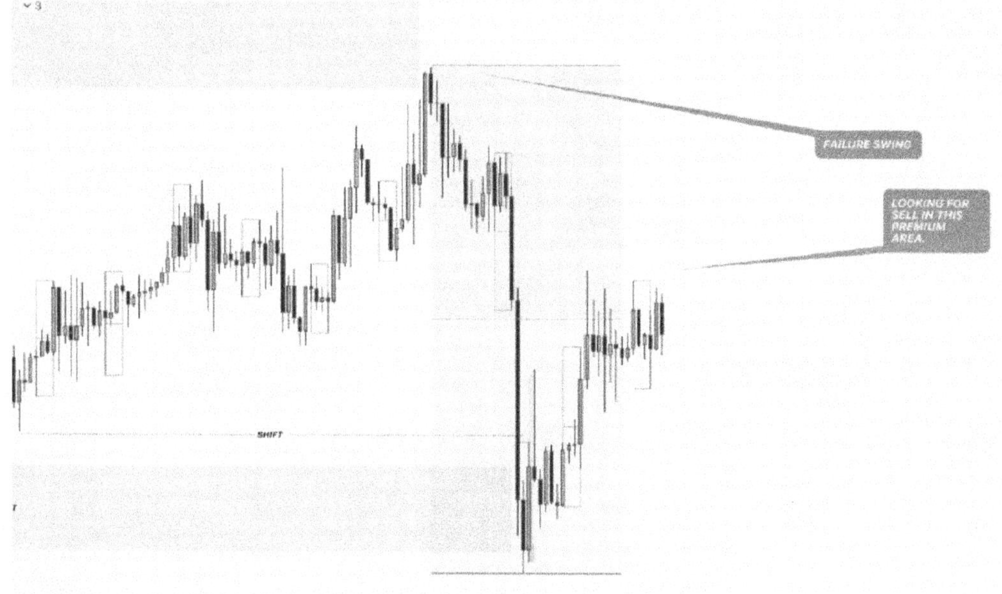

4H

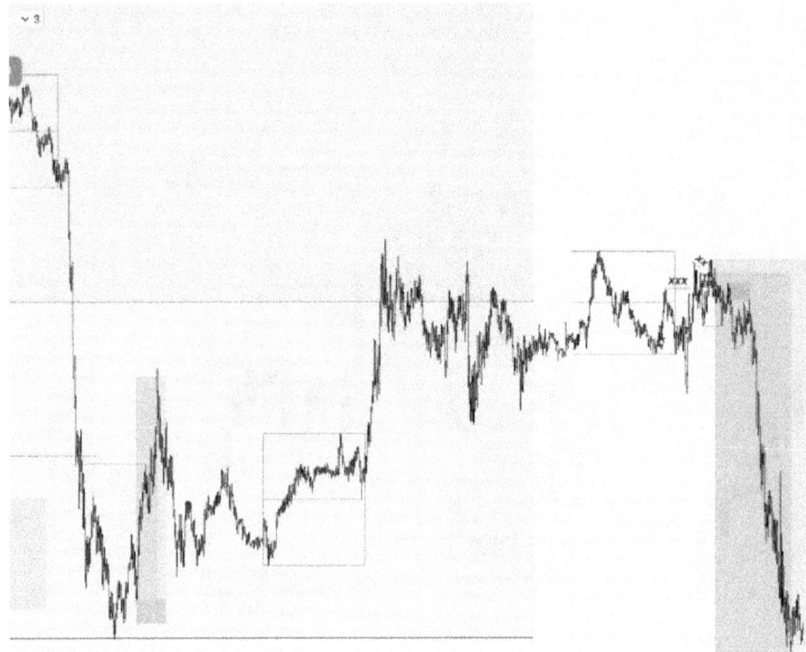

3M

I TARGET THE EXTERNAL LOW

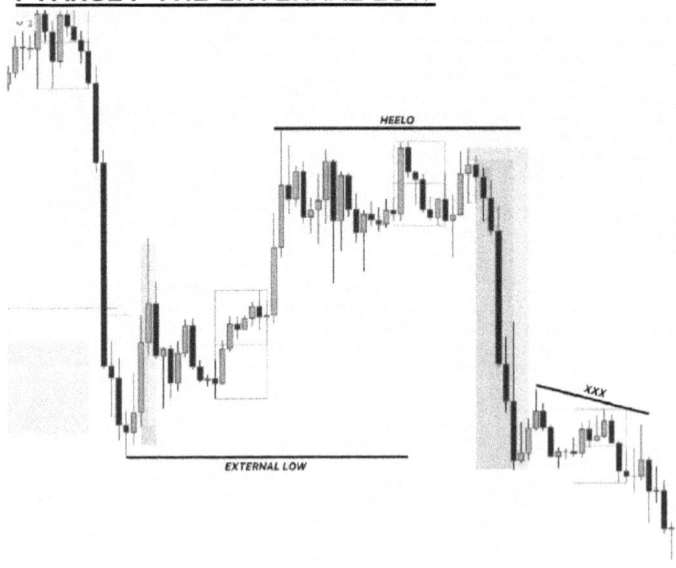

1H

3M

15M

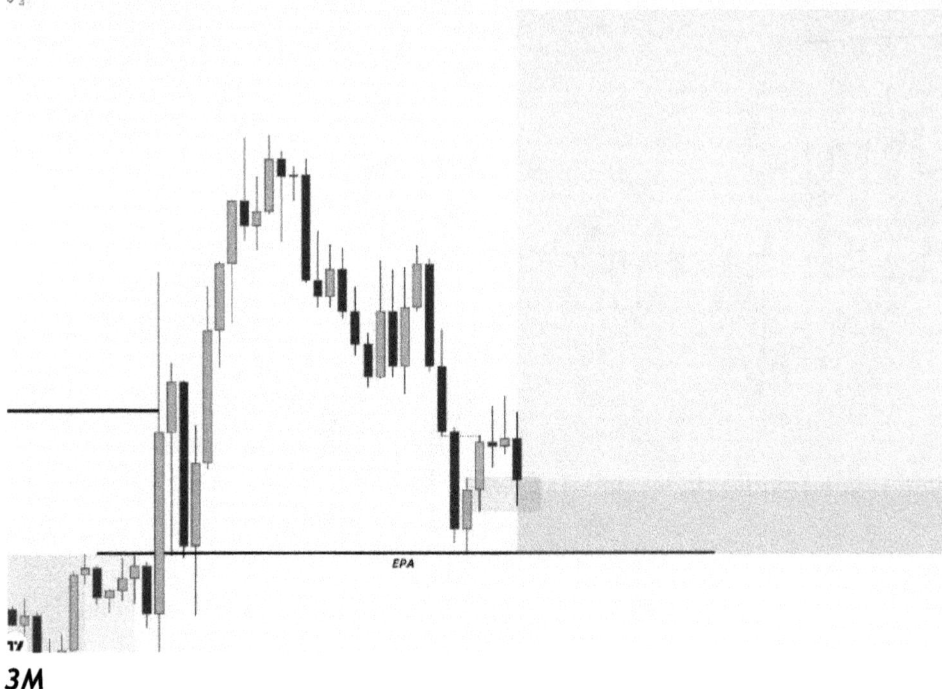

3M

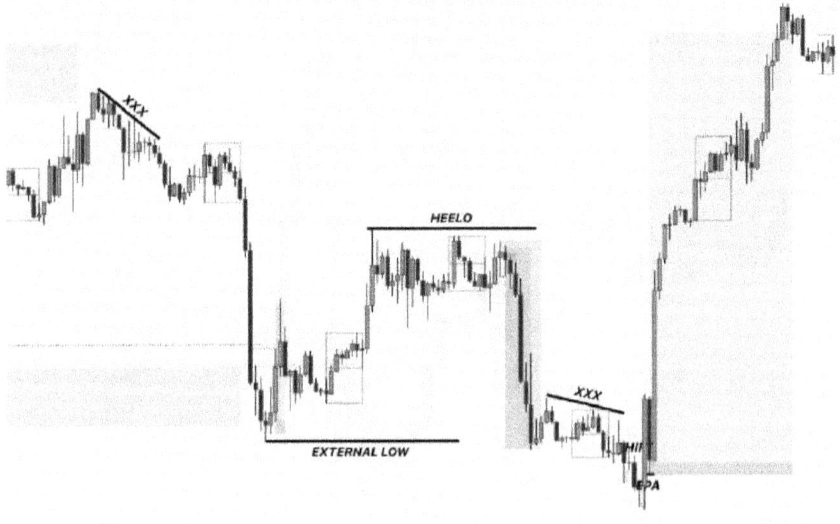

4H

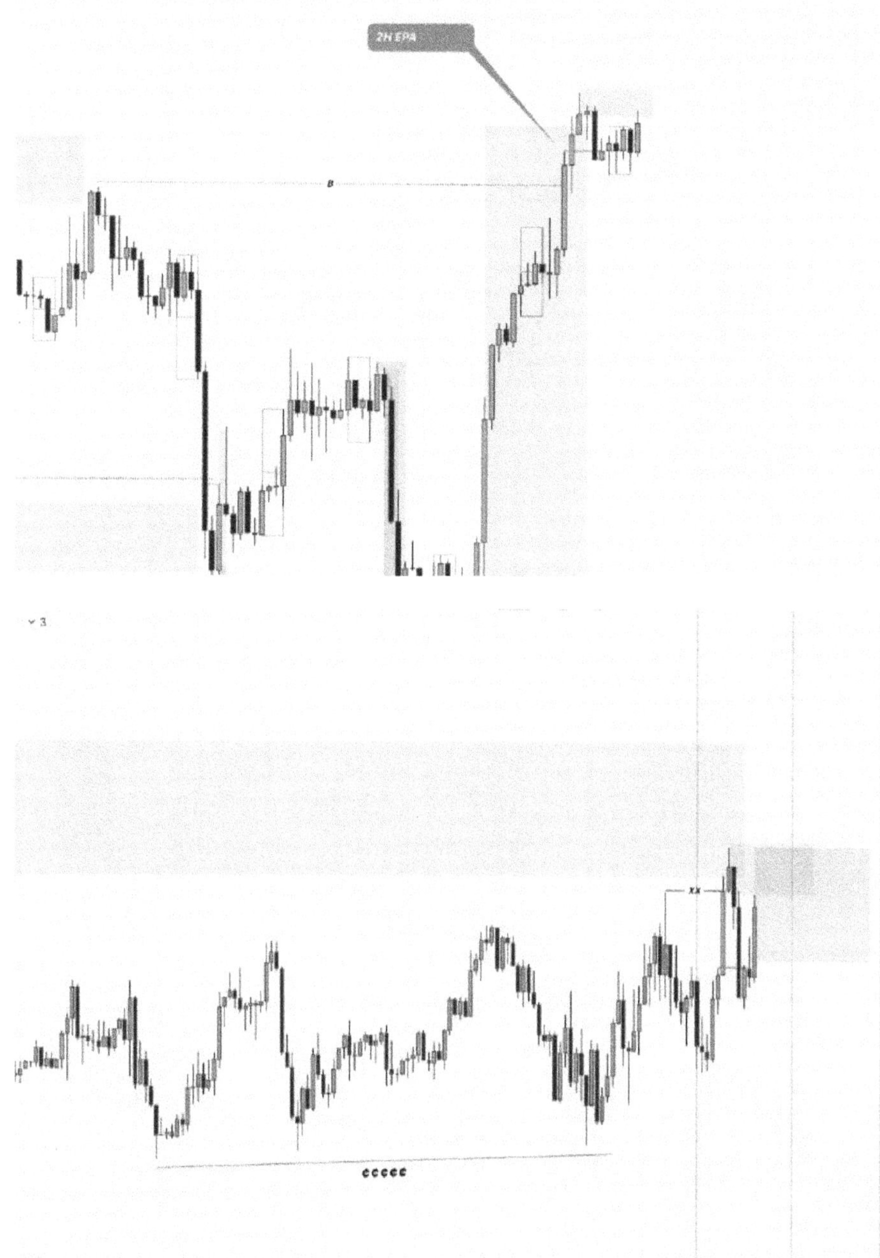

2H EPA
B
3
xx
ccccc
3M

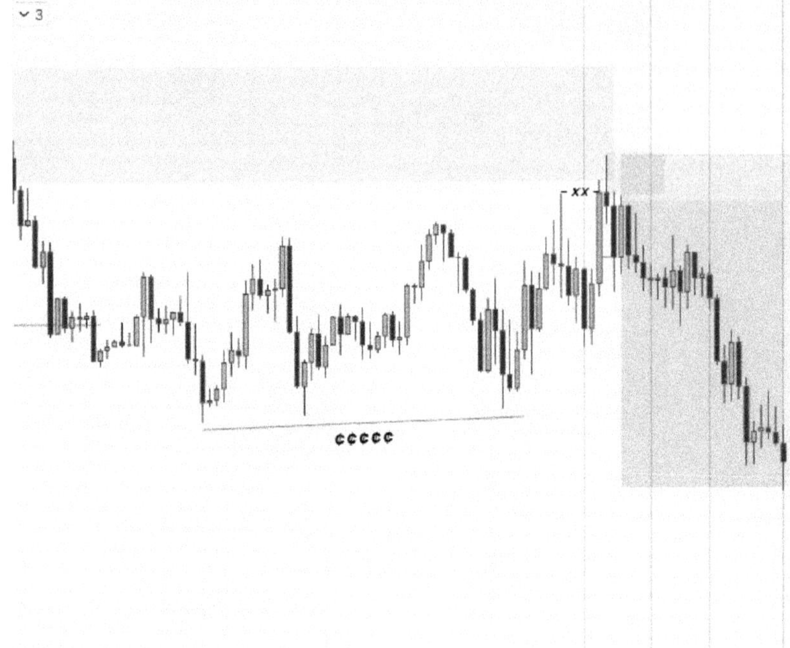

3M

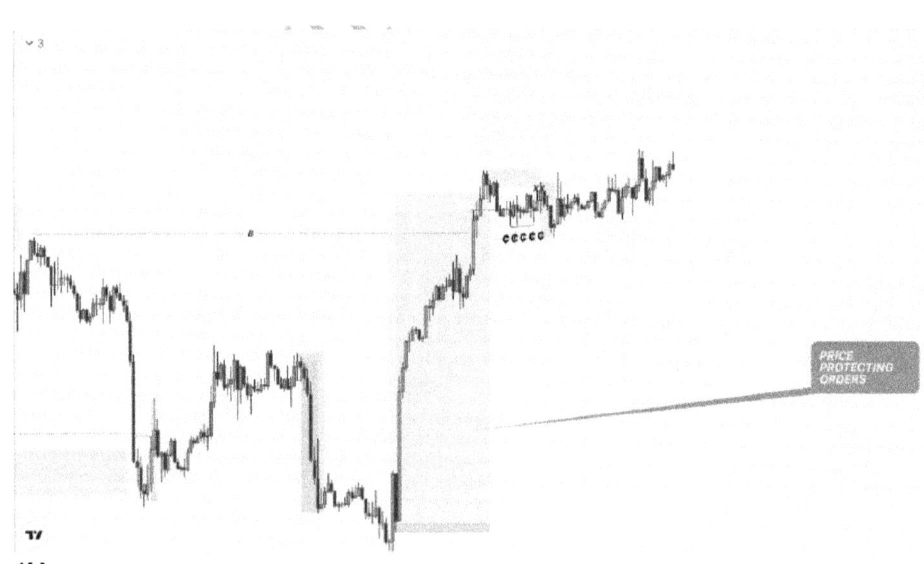

4H

As I previously mentioned, the market is like a war, and I would advise the trader not to enter into it without sufficient knowledge. My role here is to provide you with the rules for taking a trade, and not to explain each move or how to trade in this particular market. If you are trading in a ranging market, it is normal to take a risk and win. However, it is wise to wait for a clear vision before engaging in a full-fledged war. Therefore, using the knowledge we have, we should focus on a clear market structure to make it easier for you to understand. Personally, I don't need to work with market structure, but you do. As a beginner or learner, you need to use this simple method that I am providing you with.

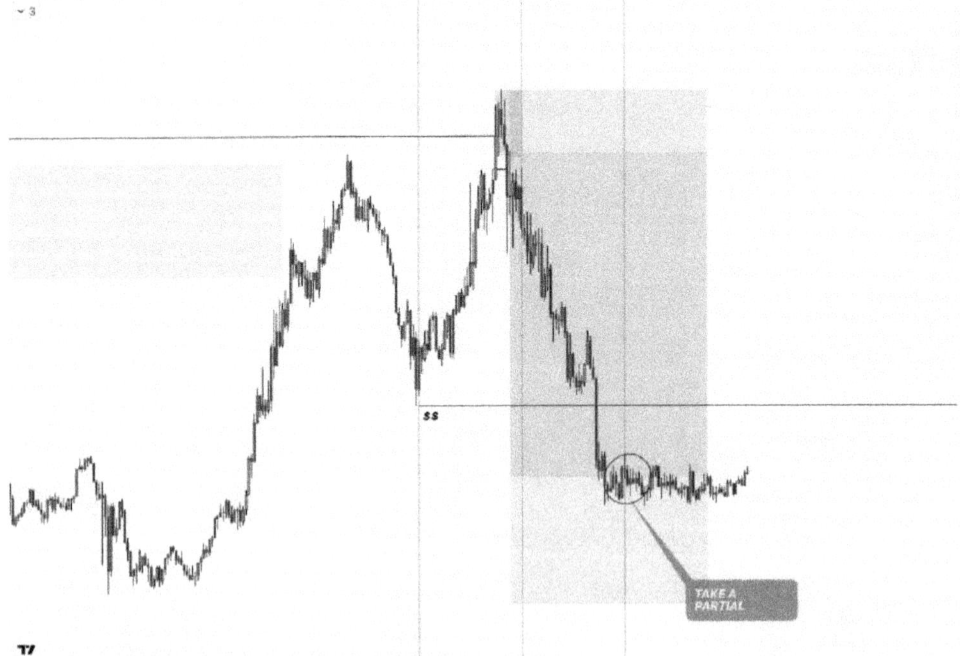
TAKE A
PARTIAL

2M

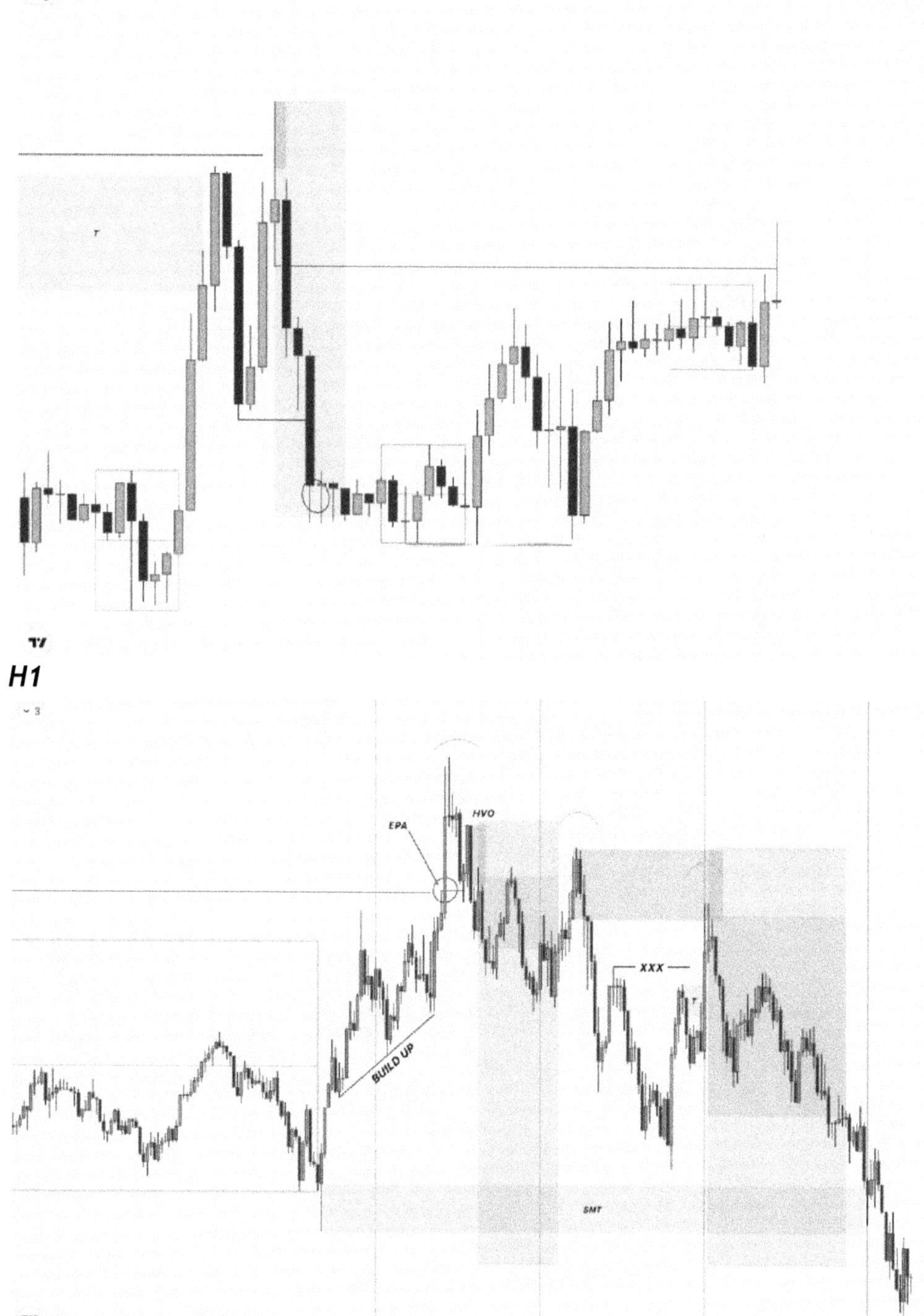

H1

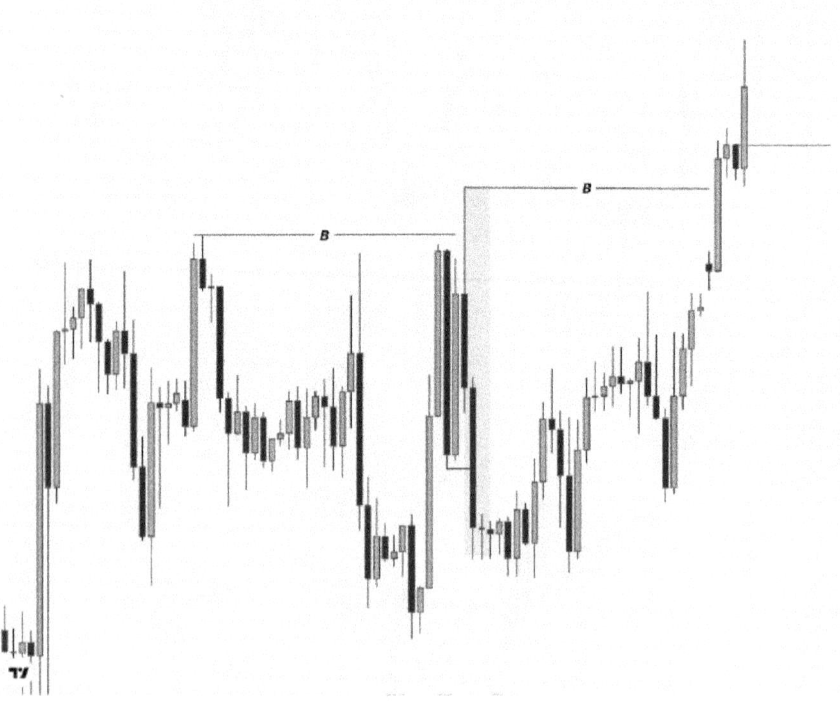
B
B

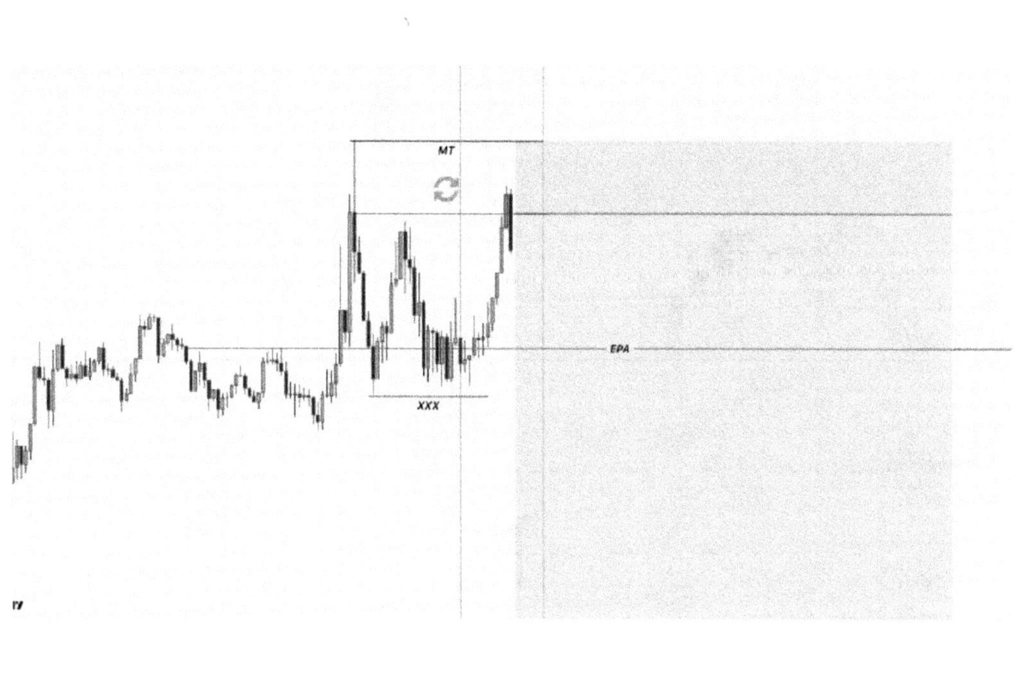

MT
XXX
EPA

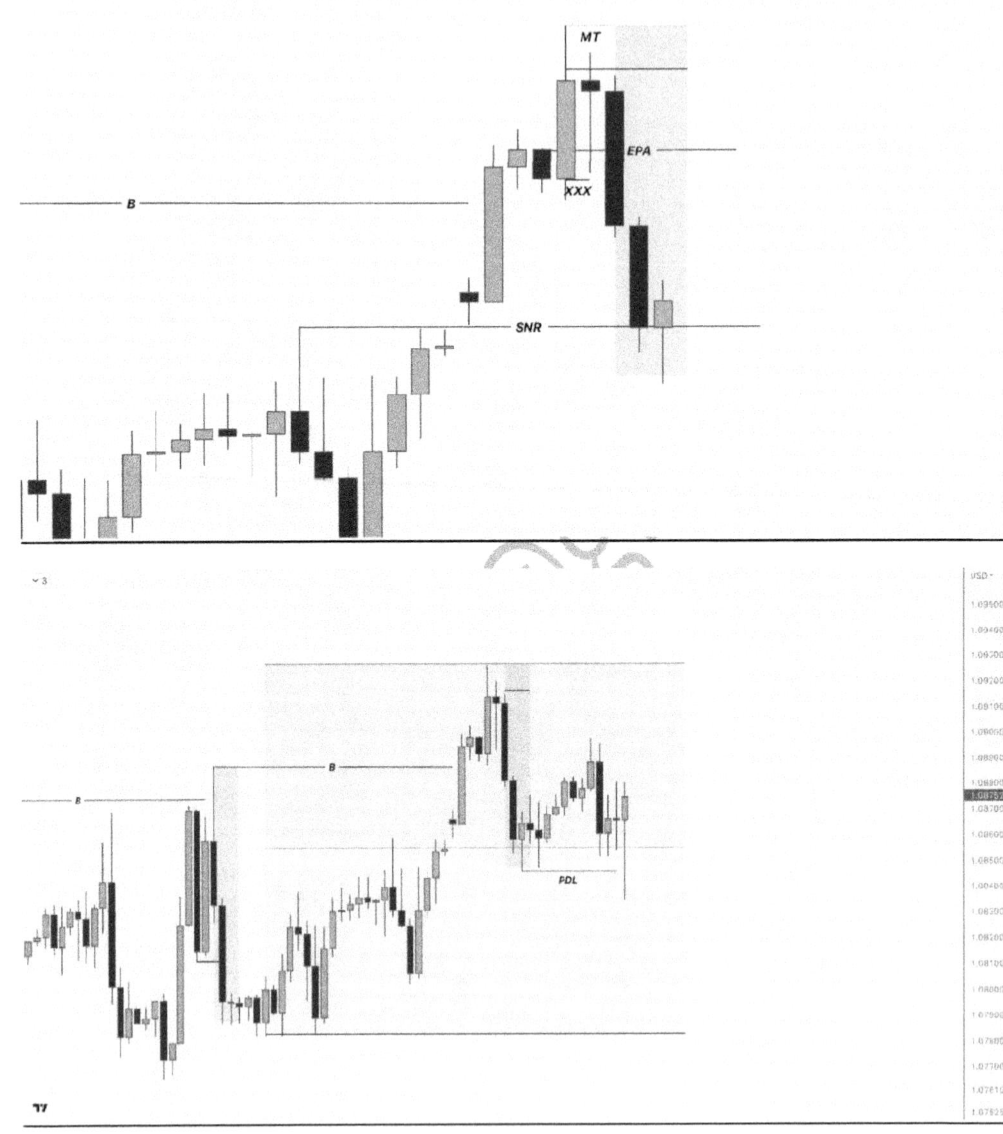

MT
EPA
B
XXX
SNR
B
B
PDL
3
USD
1.09500
1.09400
1.09300
1.09200
1.09100
1.09000
1.08900
1.08792
1.08700
1.08600
1.08500
1.08400
1.08300
1.08200
1.08100
1.08000
1.07900
1.07800
1.07700
1.07610
1.07525

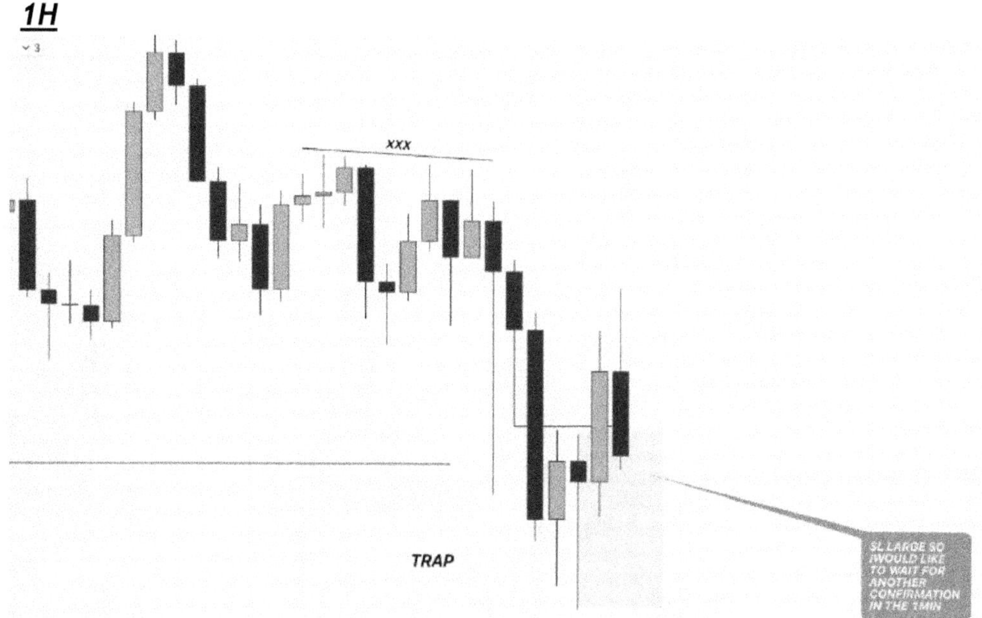
1H
3
XXX
TRAP
SL LARGE SO
I WOULD LIKE
TO WAIT FOR
ANOTHER
CONFIRMATION
IN THE 1MIN

5M

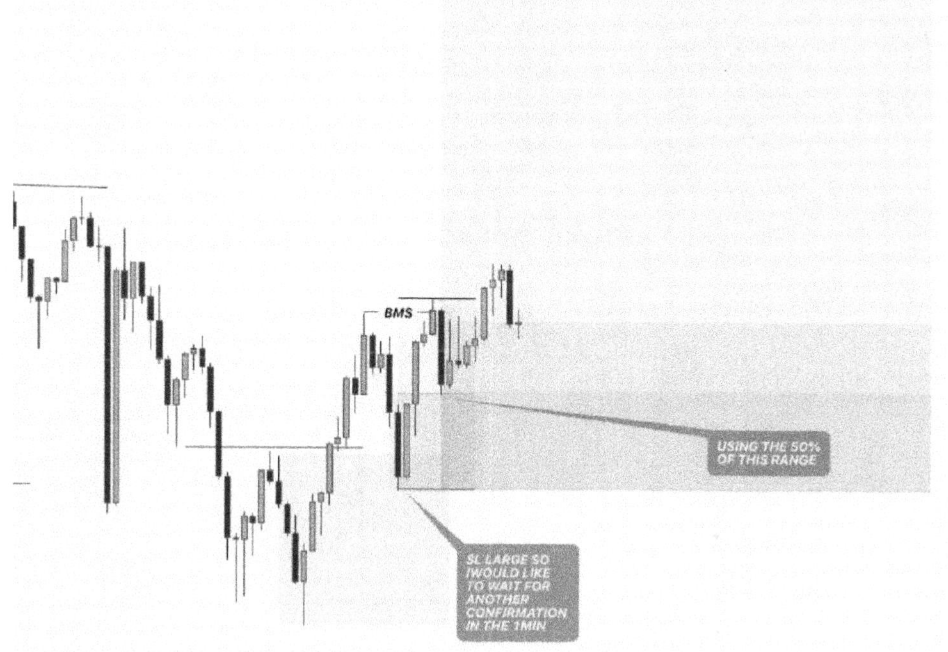
BMS
USING THE 50%
OF THIS RANGE
SL LARGE SO
I WOULD LIKE
TO WAIT FOR
ANOTHER
CONFIRMATION
IN THE 1MIN

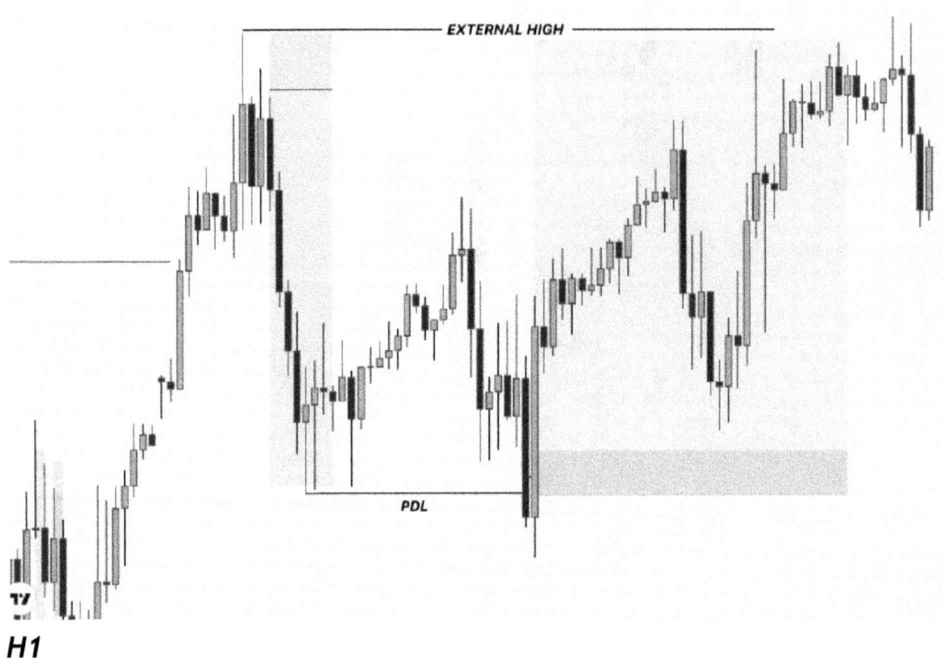

H1

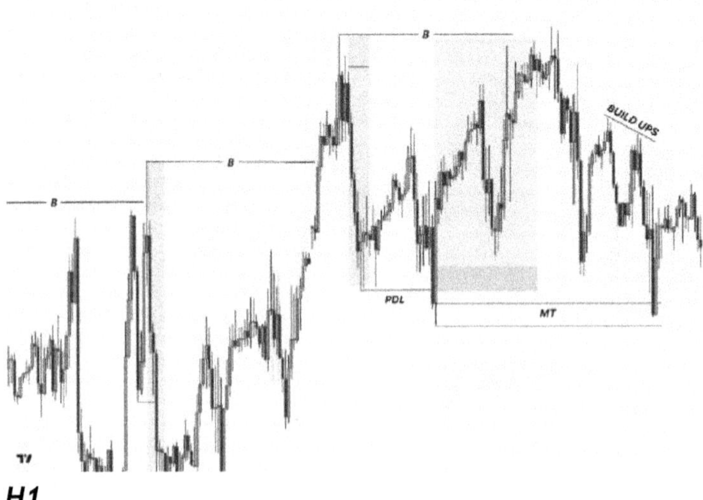

H1

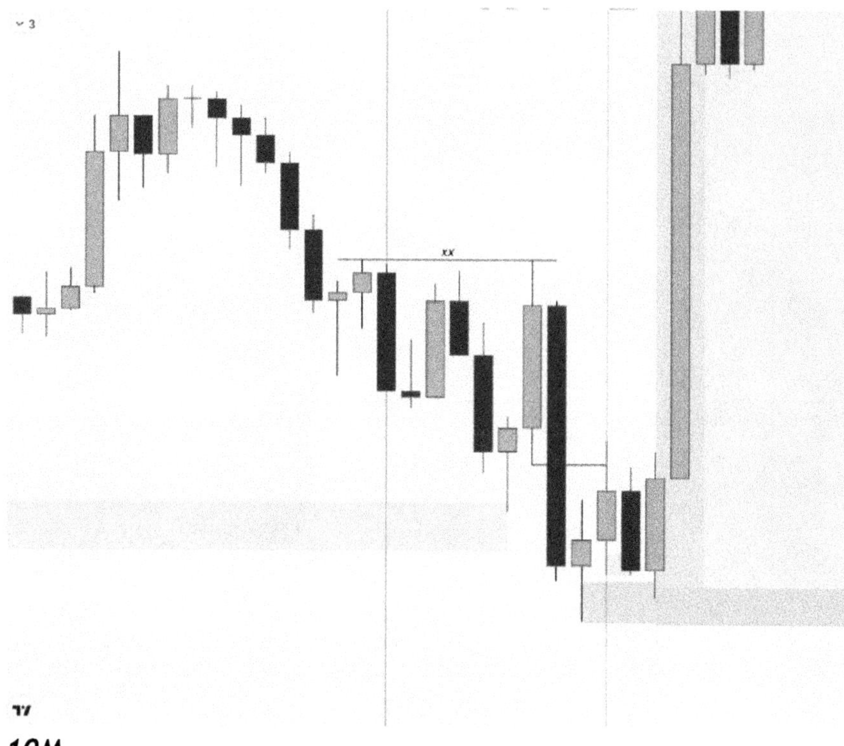
3
XX
10M

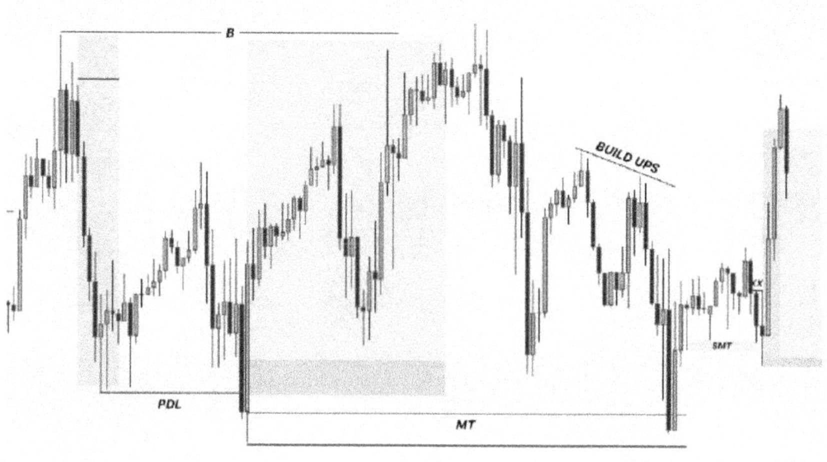
B
BUILD UPS
XX
PDL
SMT
MT
H1

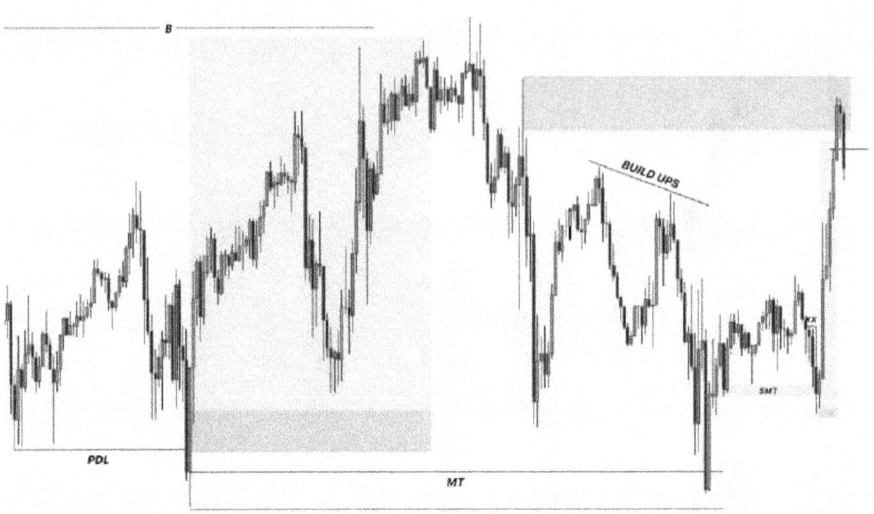

H1

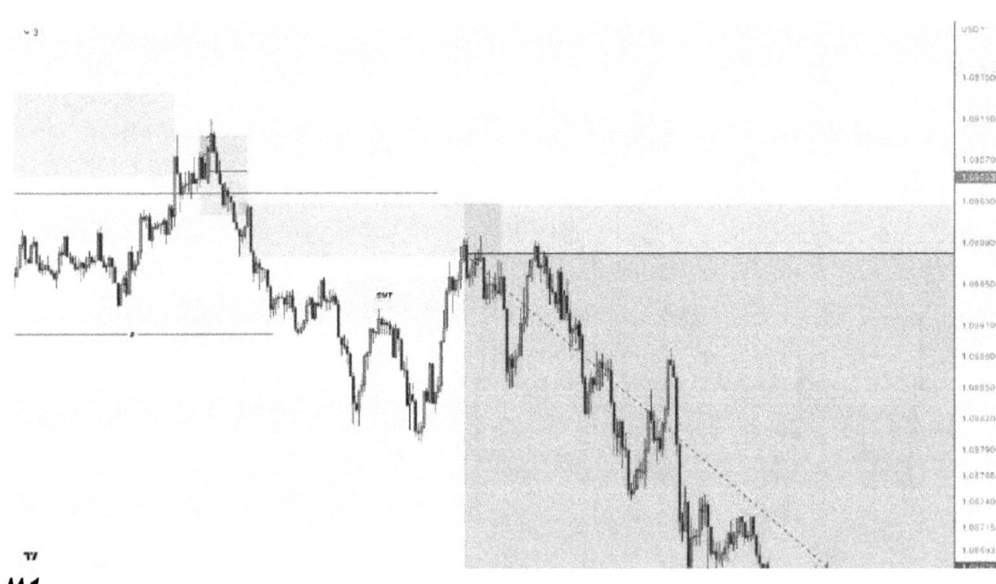

M1

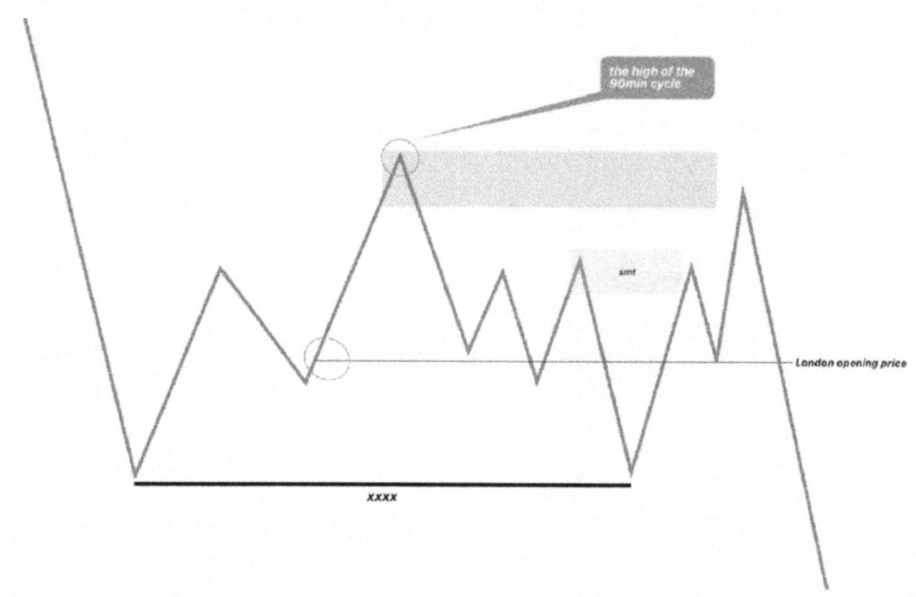

ENTRY TYPE 2

Using the session opening price to define the discount and the premium range.

Following the transfer of money every 90 minutes, a new algorithmic order   flow   needs   to   be created.

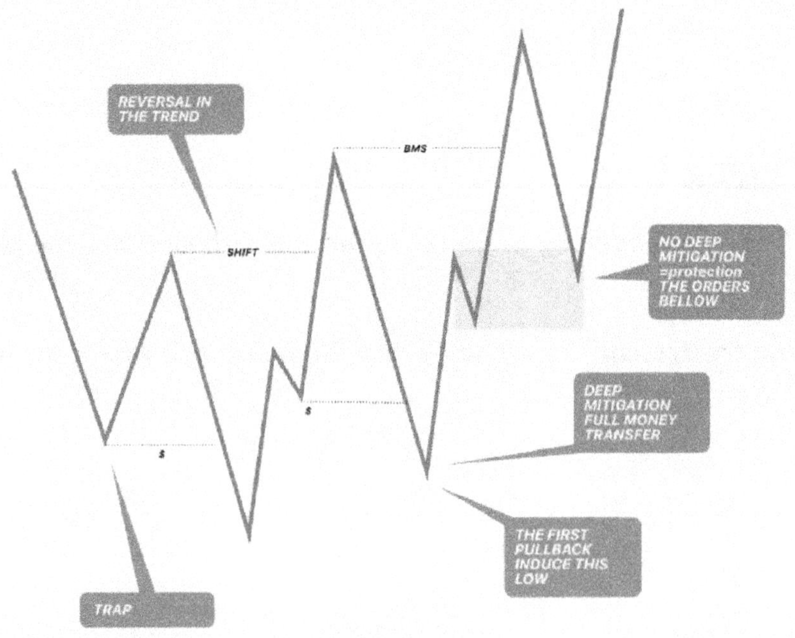

THE BEGINNING OF THE TREND

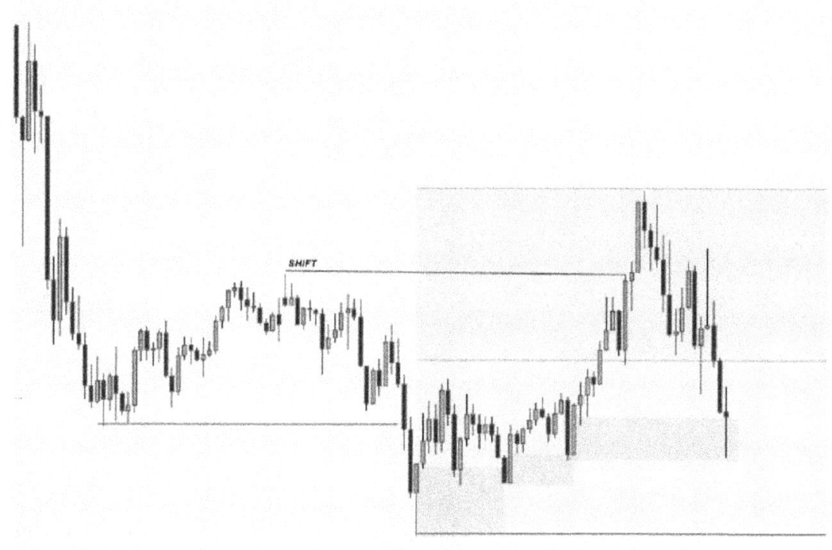

10M DEEP RETRACEMENT

1M

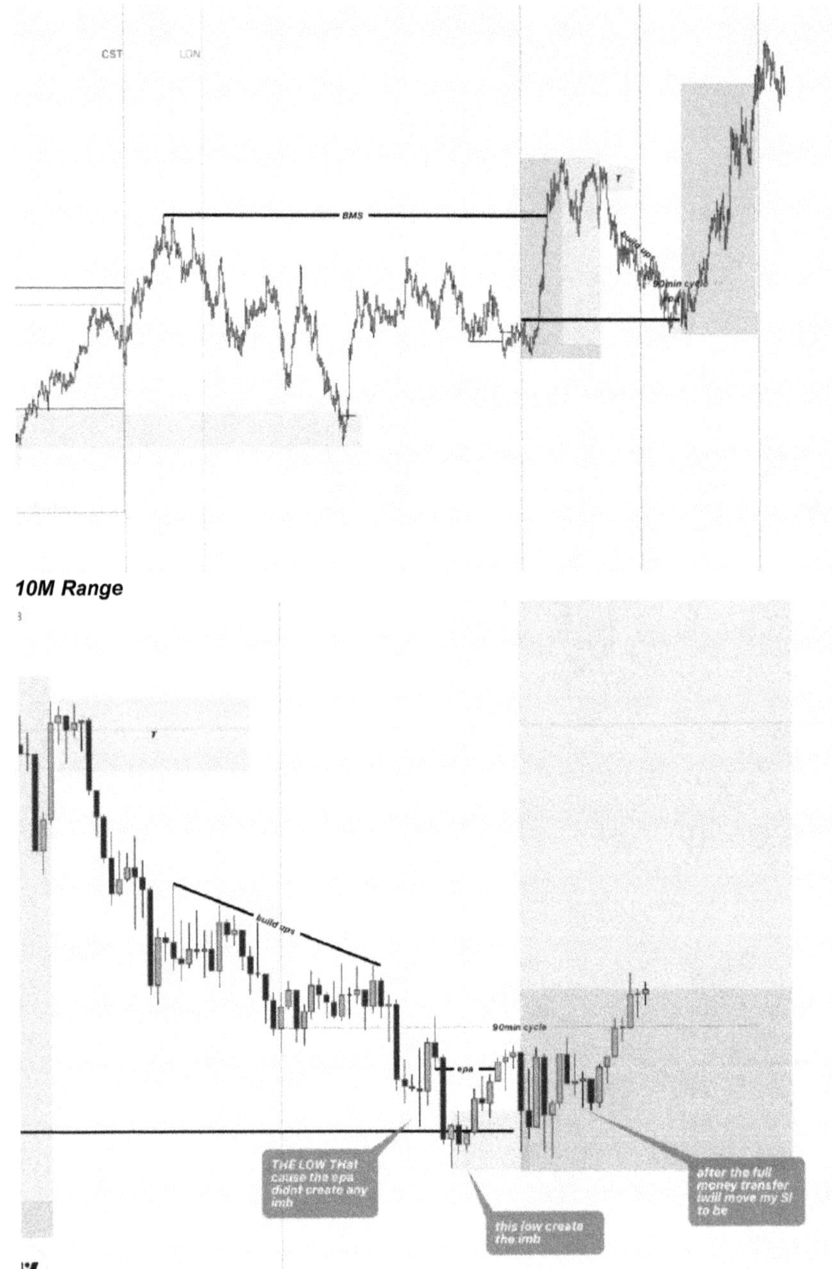

10M Range

1M Entry

15M DIRECTION

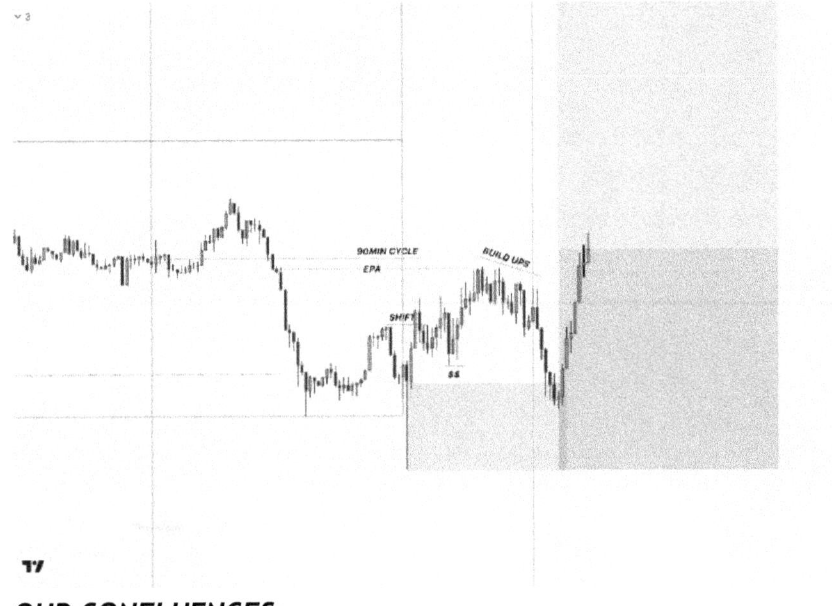

OUR CONFLUENCES:

*HTF MAJOR TRAP

*TIMING 90M CYCLE LTF ALGO ORDER

*LIQUIDITY AND BUILD UPS

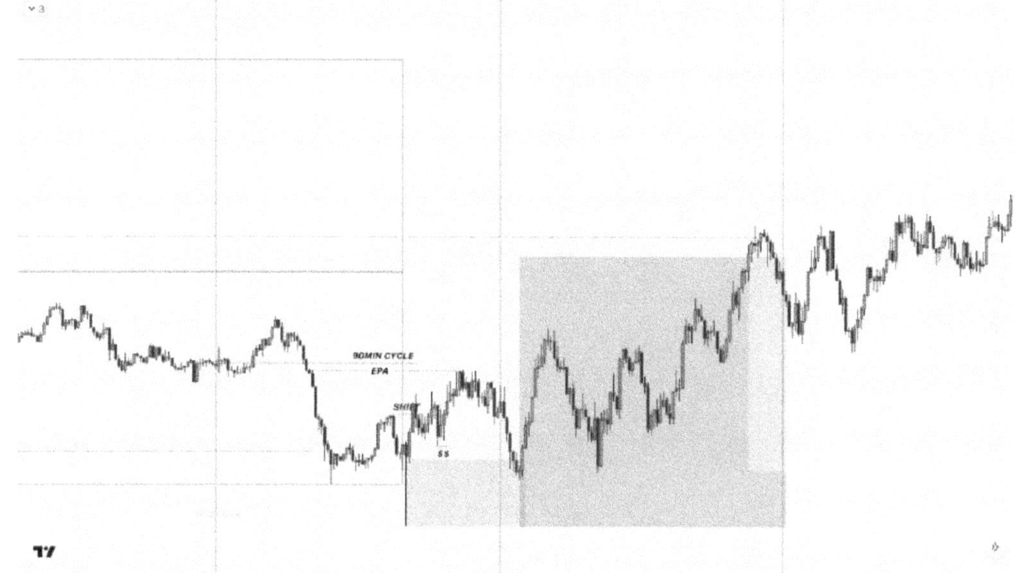

1M PULLBACK

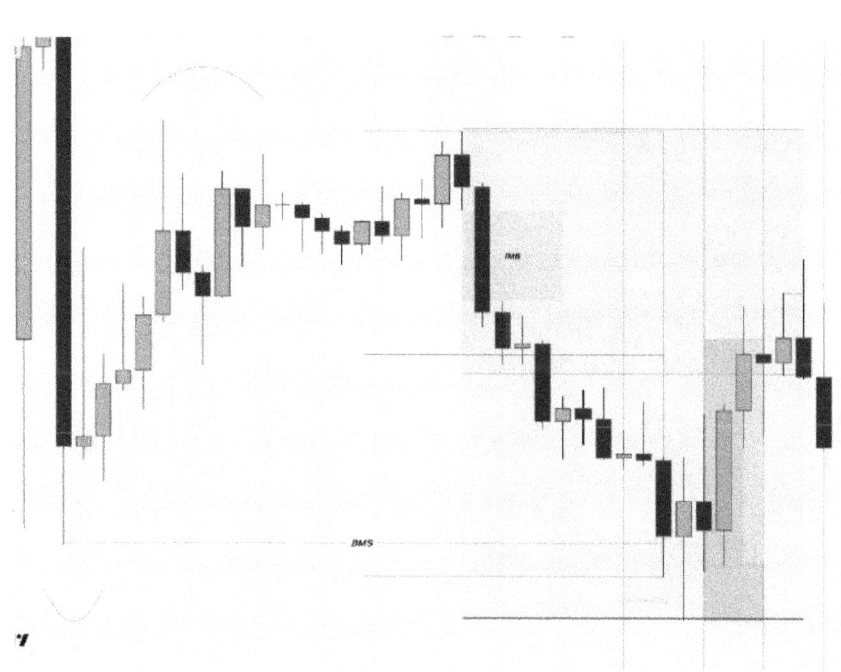

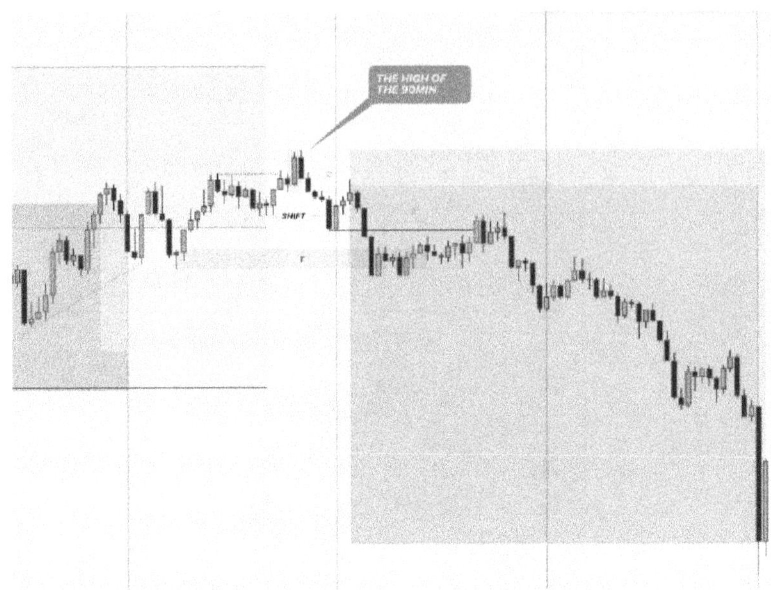

3M MONEY TRANSFER

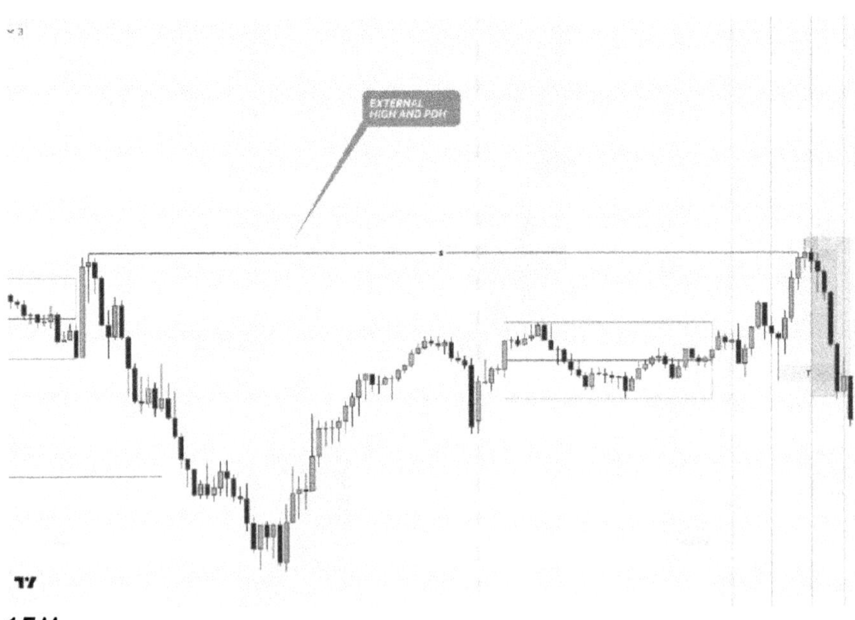

15M

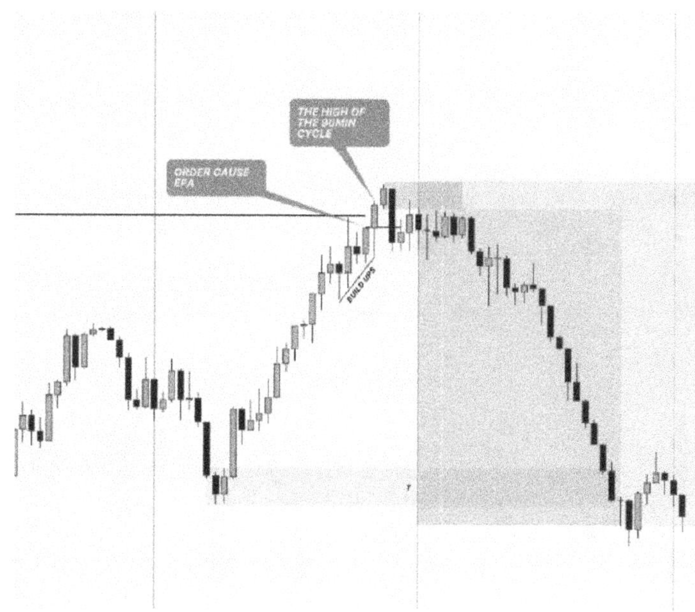
THE HIGH OF
THE 90MIN
CYCLE
ORDER CAUSE
EPA
BUILD UPS
3M

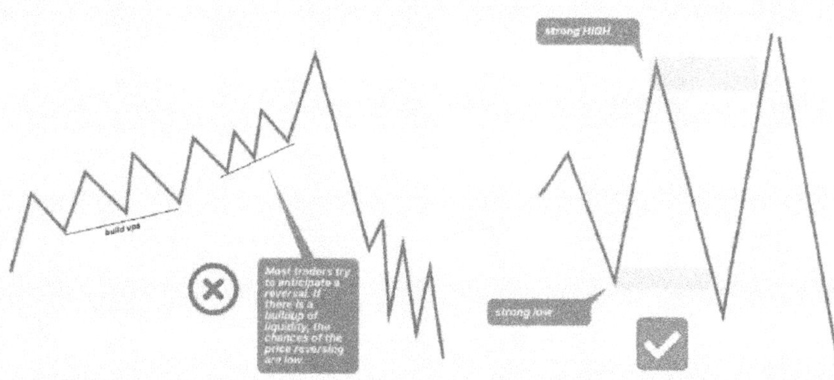
strong HIGH
build ups
Most traders try
to anticipate a
reversal. If
there is a
buildup of
liquidity, the
chances of the
price reversing
are low
strong low

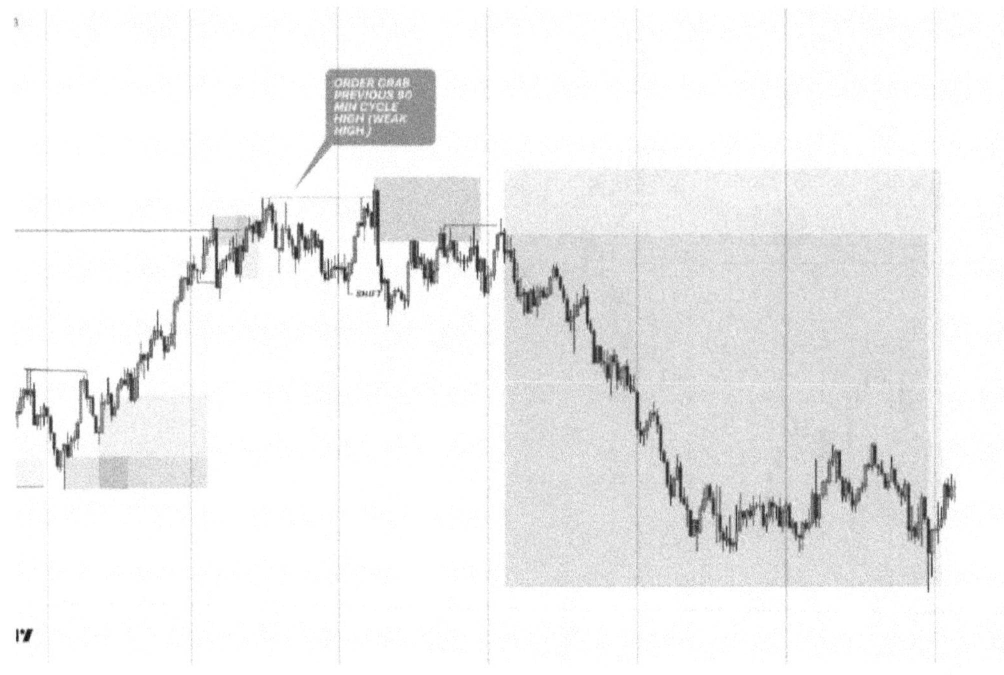

GRAB HTF STRONG POINT OF LIQUIDITY (STRON HIGH)

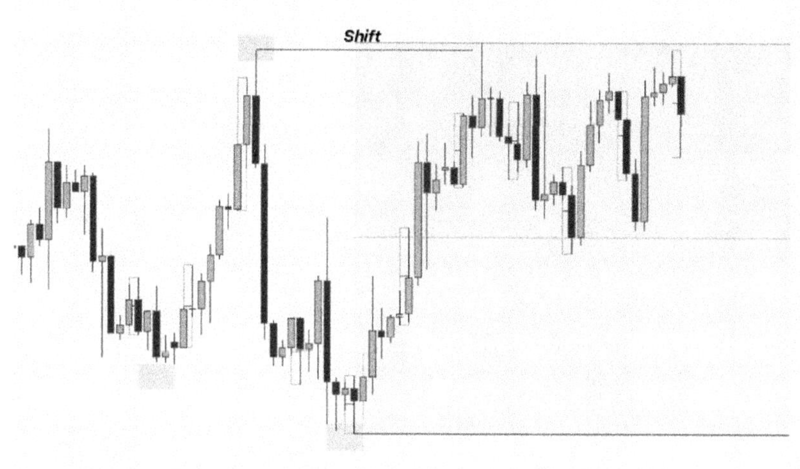

Shift

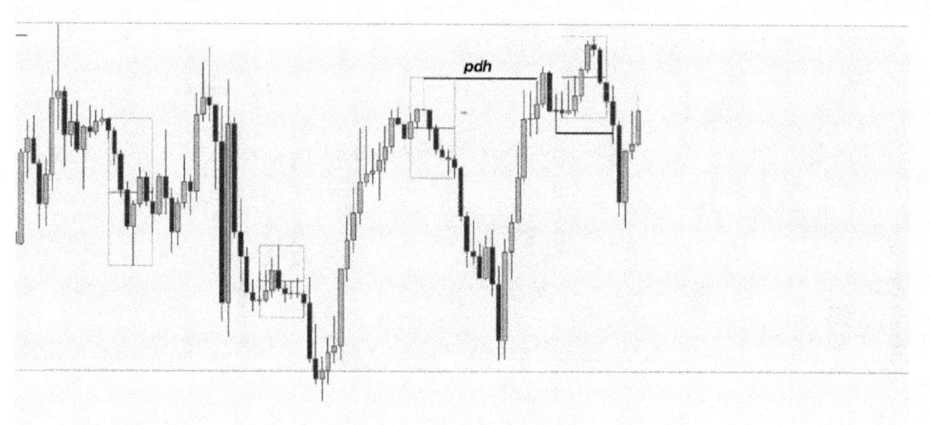

pdh

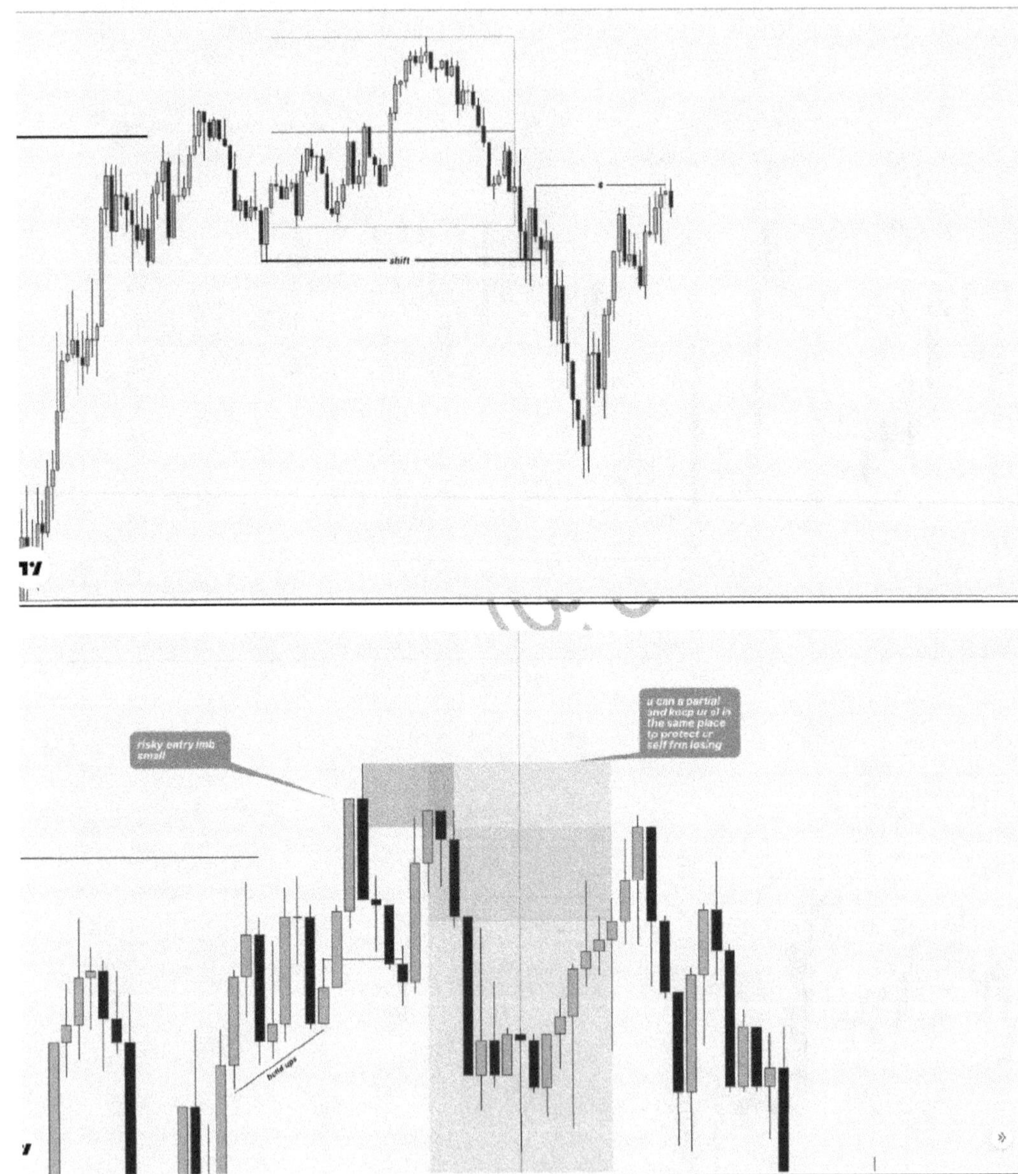
shift
risky entry imb
small
u can a partial
and keep ur sl in
the same place
to protect ur
self frm losing
build ups

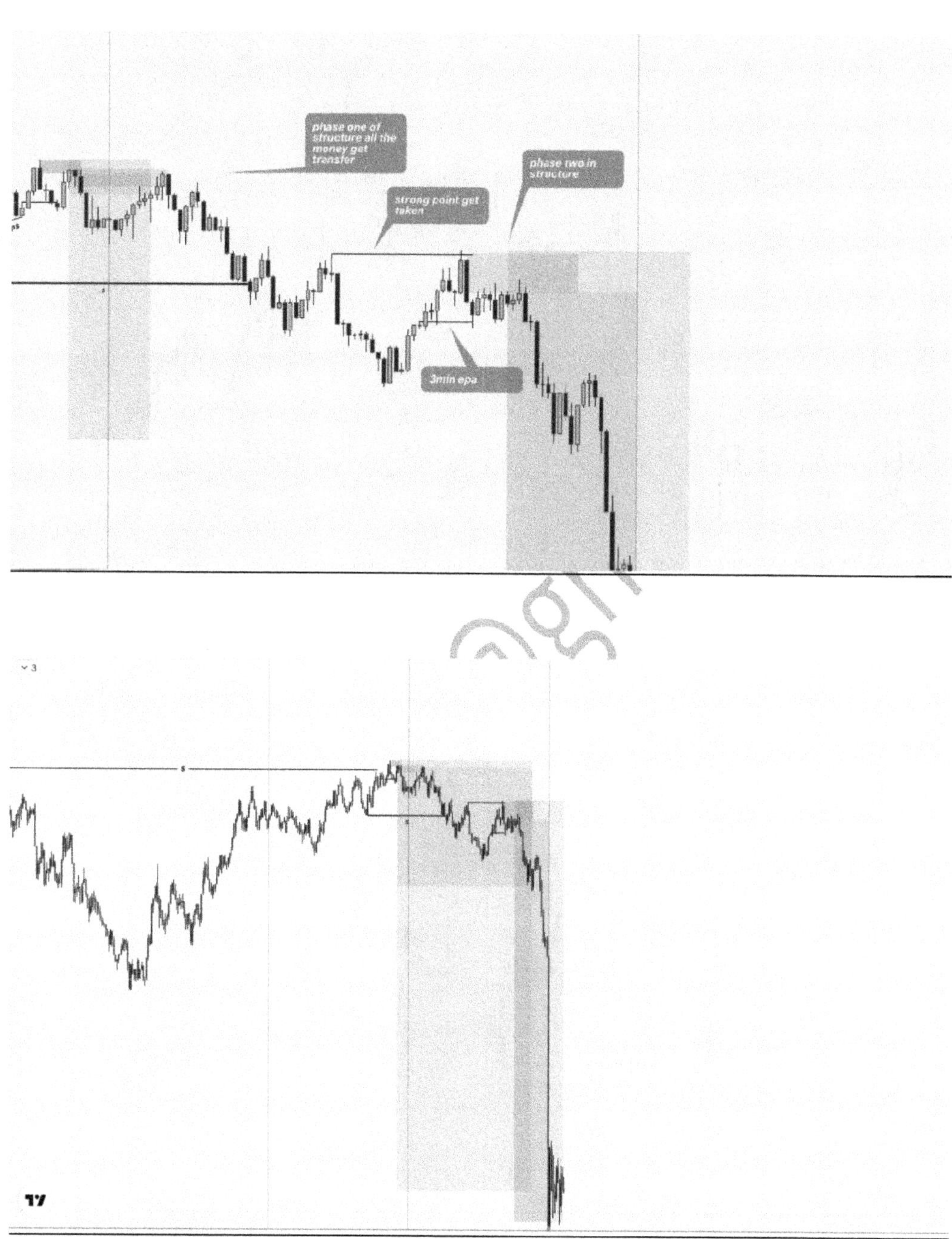
phase one of structure all the money get transfer
strong point get taken
phase two in structure
3min epa

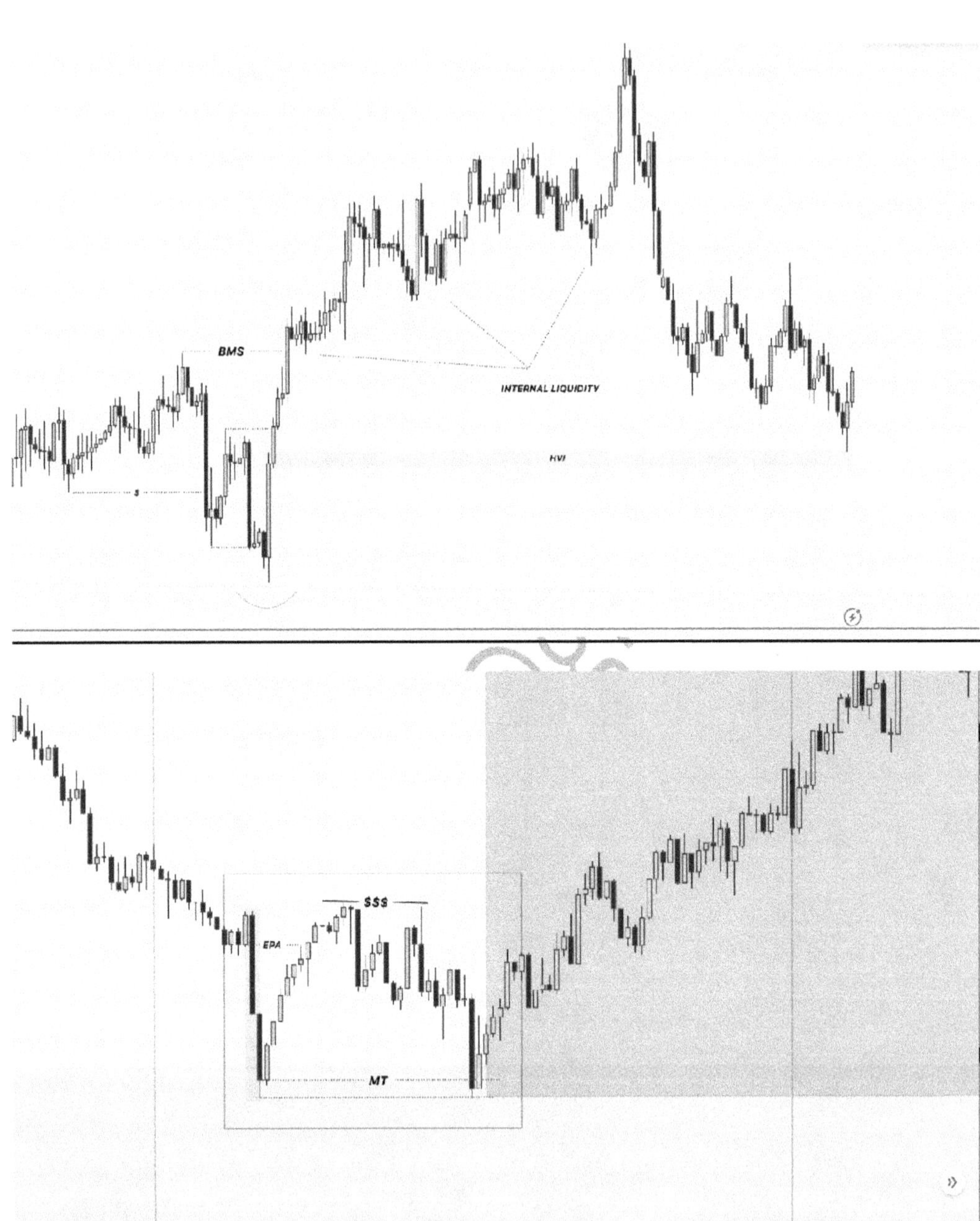

BMS
INTERNAL LIQUIDITY
HVI
$
EPA
$$$
MT

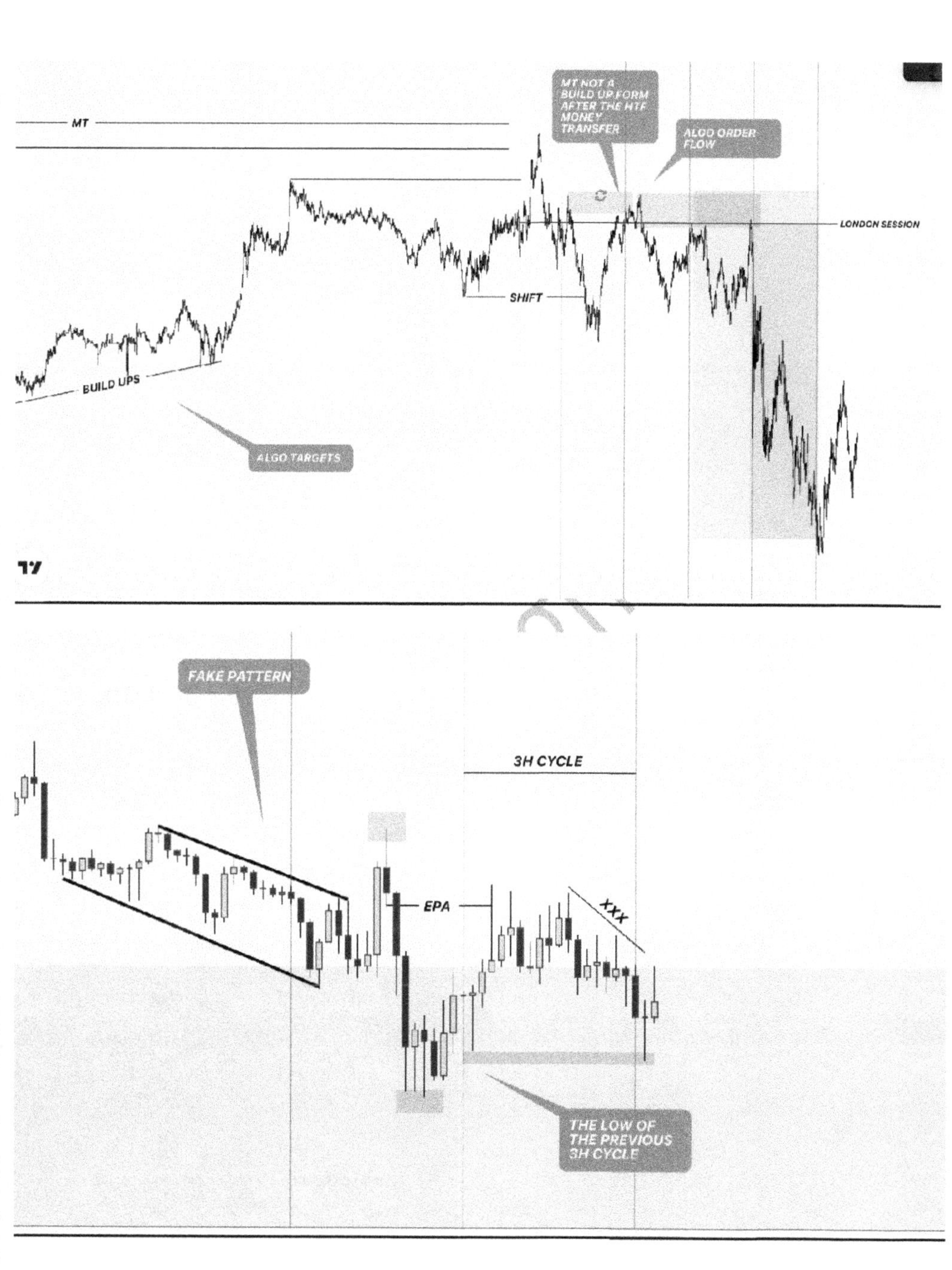

MT
MT NOT A BUILD UP FORM AFTER THE HTF MONEY TRANSFER
ALGO ORDER FLOW
LONDON SESSION
SHIFT
BUILD UPS
ALGO TARGETS
FAKE PATTERN
3H CYCLE
EPA
XXX
THE LOW OF THE PREVIOUS 3H CYCLE

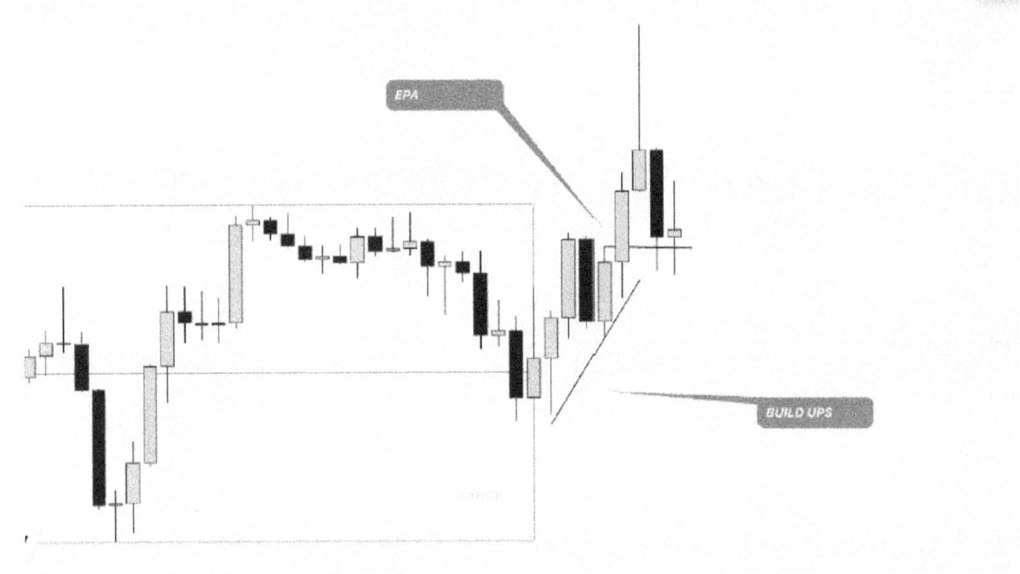
EPA
BUILD UPS

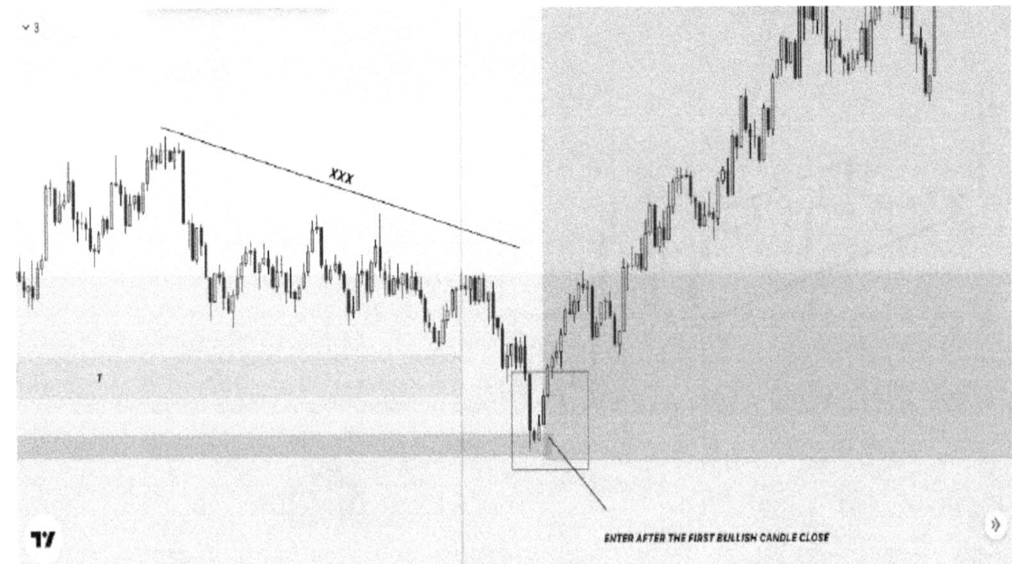
3
XXX
ENTER AFTER THE FIRST BULLISH CANDLE CLOSE

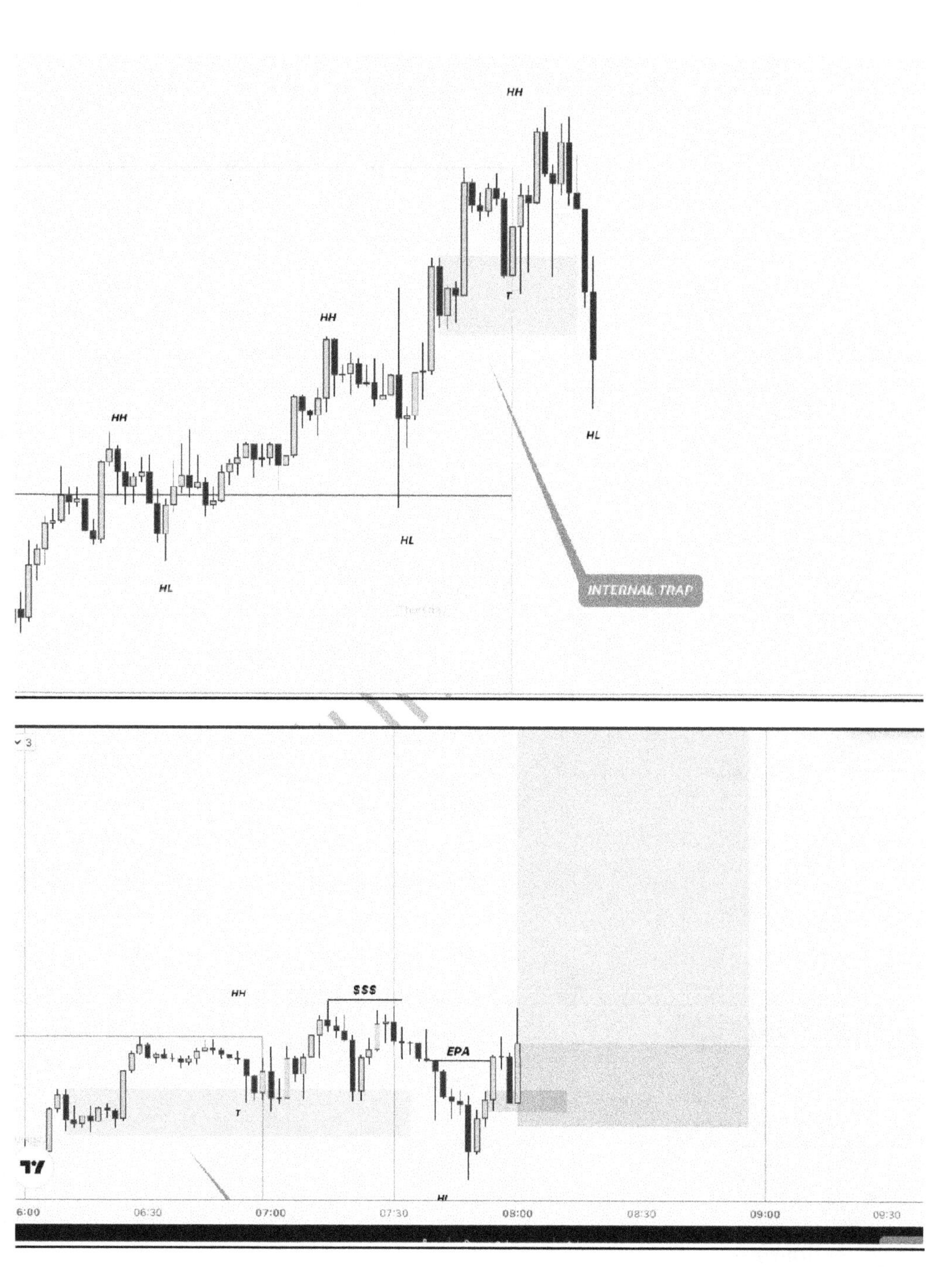

HH
HH
HH
HL
HL
HL
T
HL
INTERNAL TRAP
3
HH
$$$
EPA
T
HL
6:00
06:30
07:00
07:30
08:00
08:30
09:00
09:30

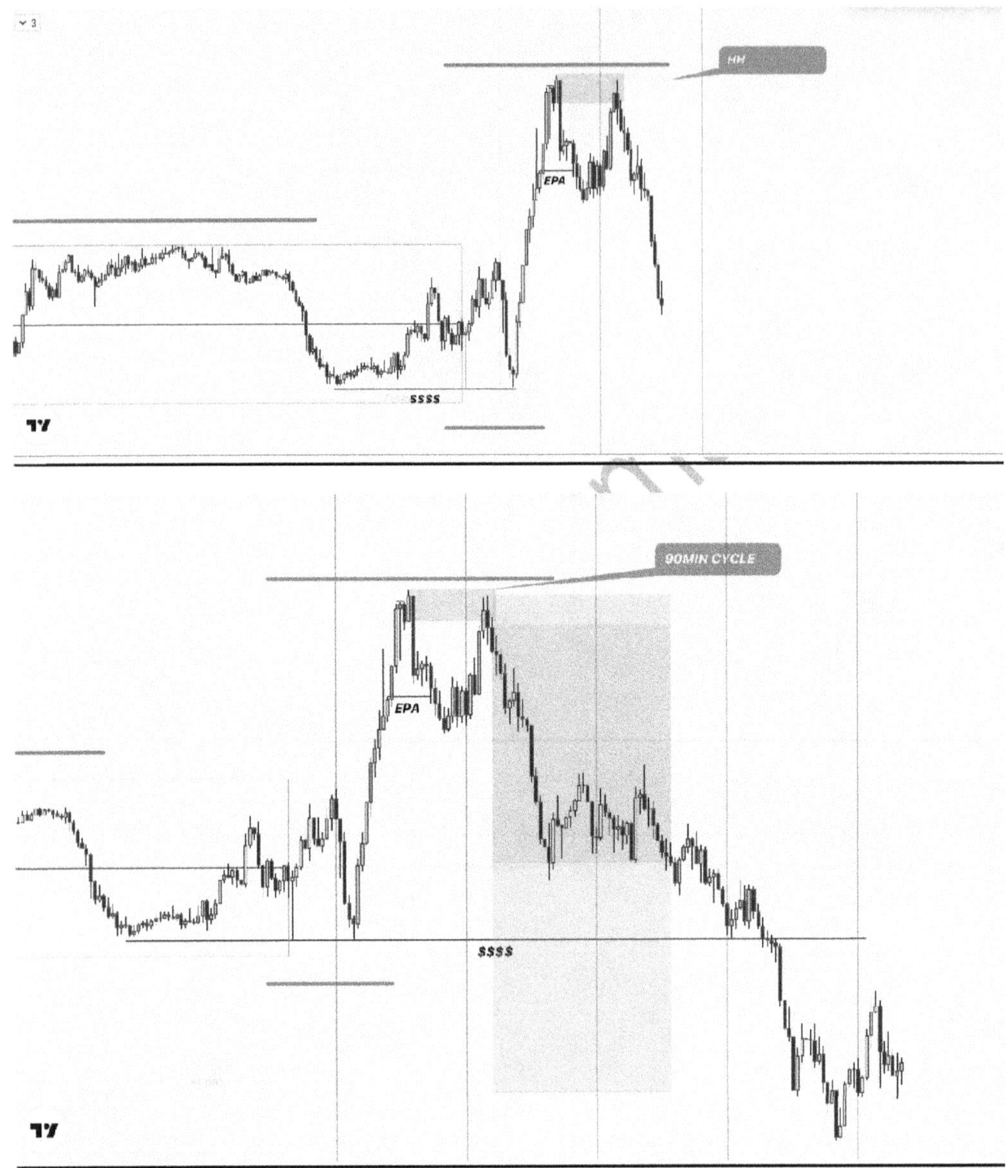

RISK MANAGEMENT

INTRADAY TRADERS

0.25% / 0.5%

Max daily drawdown 1.5%

SCALPERS

0.5% or 1%

Max daily drawdown 2%

SWING TRADERS

1% / 2%

OUR ENTRY RULES

*HTF Direction.

*Find the Trap.

*LTF entry using 90m cycle method.

*Use 4H or H1/15m/5m and 3m/1m for entries.